Archibald Porteous

A Scamper Through Some Cities of America

Being a Record of a Three Months' Tour in the United States and Canada

Archibald Porteous

A Scamper Through Some Cities of America
Being a Record of a Three Months' Tour in the United States and Canada

ISBN/EAN: 9783337187576

Printed in Europe, USA, Canada, Australia, Japan

Cover: Foto ©Andreas Hilbeck / pixelio.de

More available books at **www.hansebooks.com**

A SCAMPER

THROUGH SOME

CITIES OF AMERICA

BEING A RECORD OF A THREE MONTHS' TOUR IN
THE UNITED STATES AND CANADA.

BY

ARCHIBALD PORTEOUS.

GLASGOW:
DAVID BRYCE & SON.
1890.

PREFACE.

A TRIP across the Atlantic was a much more serious undertaking not so very many years ago than it is to-day.

Some business, and a desire to visit relations in Kalamazoo, Michigan, were the motives which induced me to cross the "herring pond," and the following narrative is published at the solicitation of friends who had read the notes which I made during the tour.

I make no pretensions to literary style, this little book being almost a *verbatim* reproduction of my diary, which was hurriedly written under many disadvantageous circumstances; and I send it forth to the world in the hope that it may prove not uninteresting to the general reader, and that the experiences of my friend and travelling companion, Mr. M——, and my own, as here recorded, may be of some service to others having a similar journey in prospect.

A. P.

33 ANN STREET, GLASGOW,
 August, 1890.

CONTENTS.

CHAPTER I.

The Voyage Out—Moville—Rough Weather—The Banks of Newfoundland—Fog—A Stowaway—Pilot, ahoy!

CHAPTER II.

Arrival at New York—Passing the Customs—The Hotel Bus Trick—Rough Streets—Magnificent Buildings—Fire-escape Ladders—The Elevated Railroad.

CHAPTER III.

Hotels—Florists' Shops—All about Flats.

CHAPTER IV.

Hoffmann House and Stewart's Luncheon Bars—Delmonico's—M —— meets an Old Friend—Brooklyn Suspension Bridge—Produce Exchange—Eastman's—St. Patrick's Cathedral—Equitable Insurance Buildings—Barnum's Show.

CHAPTER V.

Cook's Tourist Tickets—Bogus Ticket Agents—Philadelphia—Easter Saturday—Washington—A Train Ferry—Locomotives—Railroad Cars—The Train Boy.

CHAPTER VI.

Washington — Description of the City — Office-seekers — Tobacco Chewers—White House—The Capitol—Niggers—An Immersion — Novel Advertising — John Chinaman — Baltimore — Canning Factories.

CHAPTER VII.

Start for Cincinnati—The Potomac—Alleghany Mountains—Cumberland—Dining on the Cars—Cincinnati.

CHAPTER VIII.

Indianapolis—Niles—Kalamazoo—Newspaper Gossip—Some boastful Americans—"The finest in the World; Yes, Sir!"—Railway Stations—Level Crossings.

CHAPTER IX.

Kalamazoo—Americans and British Politics—The Irish Question—Presbyterian Church Service—Galesburg—Richland—Windmill Water Pumps.

CHAPTER X.

Chicago—Buildings—Train Tramcars—The Seven Sisters—Grand Pacific and Palmer House Hotels—Walking on Silver Dollars—Board of Trade—Old Hutch—The Leland House—Hustlers—Lincoln Park—The Stockyards.

CHAPTER XI.

Departure from Chicago—Arrival at Detroit—City Hall—Woodward Avenue—Windsor—Steamer on Fire—" Finest Fire Brigade in the World; Yes, Sir!"—Policemen, &c.

CHAPTER XII.

Departure from Detroit—Arrival at Niagara—The Falls—Whirlpool—Advice to Visitors.

CHAPTER XIII.

Departure from Niagara— Merriton Junction — Thorold — Electric Tramway—Hamilton—Arrival at Toronto—The University—Baseball—Toronto Island—Sunday at Toronto—Arrival at Ottawa.

CHAPTER XIV.

Departure from Ottawa—The River—Rideau Hall—Lumber Rafts—Montebello Château—Grenville—Carillon—First Railway in Canada—St. Anns—Canadian Boat Song—Lachine Rapids—Montreal.

CHAPTER XV.

Departure from Montreal—Arrival at Plattsburg—Lake Champlain—Saratoga—Boston.

CHAPTER XVI.

Boston—Baseball—Fall River—The Steamer *Providence*—Long Island Sound—Arrival at New York.

CHAPTER XVII.

Impressions of America—Methods of Government—Bribery—Politics—Administration of Justice—Jury-packing—Habits and Customs—Express Companies—Railway "Check" System—Systems of Heating—Management of Crowds—Investments in Land—Homeward Bound.

A SCAMPER

THROUGH SOME

CITIES OF AMERICA.

CHAPTER I.

The Voyage Out—Moville—Rough Weather—The Banks of Newfoundland—Fog—A Stowaway—Pilot, ahoy!

FROM St. Enoch's Station, Glasgow, to Greenock; from Prince's Pier to the deck of the Anchor line steamship *Anchoria*, and then we realized that we were not just off on a pleasure trip "doon the watter," to return the same evening. A plethora of thoughts flitted through the brain, some pleasant, some sad, but not much time was allowed for thinking. All around was bustle and confusion, passengers running hither and thither looking for missing luggage, others casting longing looks towards the shore for the faces of friends from whom they had just parted, and whom probably they would never see again. In fact the same scene was re-enacted which has been so often described before, and is occurring daily and hourly somewhere or other in this busy little world of ours. Under circumstances like these there is an infinite amount of pathos in that one expressive word—" Farewell."

At 9 p.m. we proceeded slowly down the beautiful Firth of Clyde, which, however, was not particularly lovely on this occasion, as it was raining and the fog so dense that the shores on either side were barely visible.

At seven o'clock next morning we dropped anchor about a mile off Moville, in Lough Foyle, on the north coast of Ireland. Londonderry is sixteen miles distant, and a large ferry-boat was expected to bring from there over 300 Irish emigrants, bound for the New World in our ship. We had quite a crowd already on board, but the accommodation in modern ocean-going steamships appears to be unlimited. Meantime we had to await the arrival of these poor folks, so in the interval a few of the cabin passengers went ashore to inspect the prettily-situated little town of Moville.

A strong current was running up Lough Foyle, and a stiff breeze blowing down, which made the sea decidedly "lumpy," consequently it was rather ticklish work getting into the small boat, as we had to go over the side of the ship by means of a rope-ladder. One passenger, Mr. W. P——, sent us into fits of laughter, by the performance of some extraordinary, and, I should imagine, hitherto never attempted acrobatic feats during his descent. He appeared to think the proper way to use a rope-ladder was to throw his legs around it, and, while he was suspended thus in mid-air, he looked exactly as if he felt his last hour had come. However, he held on bravely, and eventually dropped safely into the jolly-boat.

Immediately on getting ashore we were surrounded by a crowd of the most impertinent, importunate, blarney-talking nuisances, in the shape of hack-drivers, that we ever met anywhere. These fellows—"jarvies" they call them—would not take "No" for an answer. Two of them, each leading his horse and car, followed my companion and myself for fully a mile, and it was only when, as a last resource, we indulged in some rather strong language, that we finally got quit of them. After a six-mile walk, we returned on board about one o'clock, and soon thereafter the emigrants from Derry came alongside. What an assortment they were! Old men and women, young lads and lasses —the latter mostly with no hats, only shawls thrown over their heads—and children and babies. And then "the anchor's weighed"—the ferry steamer's ropes were cast off, and the gangways closed. Anon the boatswain's whistle piped shrilly above the general din, the throbbing screw slowly revolved, and the great leviathan forged steadily ahead through the driving wind and rain. . . . A few hours later we were pitching and rolling and ploughing our way through the billows and over them, out of sight of land, and fairly "off" on our voyage to New York.

I am obliged to draw a curtain over the events of half a week, so far as I am personally concerned, owing to circumstances over which I had no control! During two days a high sea was running, the next it was blowing a gale from the N.W., with heavy squalls, which heeled us over to the gunwales, accompanied by showers of hail and rain. All the passengers were below one entire day, owing to so much water coming over. Most of us were " pretty bad," and those of our number who were not affected with *mal de mer* were very attentive to their sick fellow-voyagers.

A service was held in the saloon on Sunday, conducted by Mr. H—— K——, of Hartford, Conn. I was lying on a couch in the drawing-room, which is in reality the gallery round the dining saloon, whilst they sang, " I to the hills will lift mine eyes." Although I did not wish to be irreverent, I could not resist thinking at the time that I would have given a good deal to have been able to lift my eyes as high as the table!

We passed two or three ships within twenty-four hours after leaving Moville; in one case the tops of the masts only being visible above the horizon.

A dense fog was entered as we approached the Banks of Newfoundland. They are so called because all over this region the depth of the Atlantic is only about thirty or forty fathoms, so that a ship could easily anchor if necessary. The fog horn was sounded every thirty seconds during the whole night, until a S.W. breeze arose about seven in the morning, when the fog rolled away like a curtain, and the sun shone out. I was on deck at the time, and was glad to be so fortunate as to witness such a novel and beautiful sight.

My portmanteau and M——'s hatbox had an almost perpetual waltz round our little cabin night and day since we left Moville. Sometimes they tired of being confined in the limited area at their disposal, and gambolled playfully along the passage outside. Other passengers' luggage played the same "fantastic tricks," all the state-room doors being kept open to admit of as much ventilation as possible (curtains only being used, to secure privacy), and the corridor was evidently the favourite playground of these sea-sick packages.

No one could wish for better fare than that provided on board the *Anchoria*. Breakfast was served at 8 a.m., luncheon at 1 p.m., and dinner at 6 p.m. Up to this particular time I had had no appetite for meat, drink, or tobacco !!!

The ship's clock is put back about half an hour every day on the Western passage, so that if we were to arrive in New York at 12 noon my watch, Glasgow time, should indicate 5 p.m. On the return voyage, of course, this process is reversed.

Most of the saloon passengers were standing on deck one morning holding a " council of war " as to whether we should indulge in a game of rope quoits or shuffleboard, when Mr. Mathieson, the purser, came along and, with a merry twinkle in his eye, informed us that a stowaway had appeared. Great interest was evinced by all of us in the unfortunate little rascal. Questions as to where he had hidden himself, how old he was, and so on, were on every tongue. When our surmises and inquiries were exhausted, Mr. Mathieson burst into a cheery laugh and informed us that one of the Irish emigrant girls had just given birth to a fine boy, and both were doing well! The hat was passed round our little group, and as a result 20s. was handed to the purser for the benefit of the poor woman. On a second appeal being made later over a wider circle, more than £5 was collected for her altogether.

The deck was now daily crowded with passengers, who had all nearly recovered from sickness. A strong head wind had by this time arisen, which changed the motion of the vessel from a roll to a pitch—a great improvement. The sun shone out brightly, but its warmth was tempered with a pleasant breeze.

There was a piper on board who, when he could find room on deck (the steerage passengers now daily spread themselves all over it like herrings on a plate), marched up and down blowing his best.

By and by another dense fog was entered; we couldn't see ten yards in front of the ship. The fog horn sounded every thirty seconds, the engines were slowed down to half speed, and then stopped altogether. At this moment the saloon passengers were present by invitation at a concert and dance in the intermediate cabin, so we all crowded up on deck to learn what was wrong. Another steamer was not far off, sounding her fog horn too. Unable to see anything, we waited patiently the turn of events. It was rather exciting, but everybody kept remarkably cool. After a short but anxious interval we steamed ahead again at full speed, having exactly ascertained the direction and distance, so far as hearing could indicate, of the other vessel, which was on our starboard side steering in an easterly direction. The fog lasted during the night, so the horn was kept blowing at the usual intervals till five o'clock in the morning, when it cleared away. The cheery voices of the watch sang out at each half hour bell. The for'ard watch cried "All lights burnin' brightly," the mid-watch "All's well"—five seconds on each word—and the watch "aft" repeated in the same musical fashion the refrain "All's well." It was very pretty, and in circumstances like these just recorded very reassuring to the wakeful voyager down below.

One of our passengers, a Canadian, Mr. P——, of Quebec, did not try to make himself agreeable to the rest of us, with the result that a good deal of chaff went on at his expense. He wore an enormous "Tam o' Shanter" for a day or two, but " really if he intended to pass himself off as a Scotchman at the other side, we ought to know the reason why he invested in such a hideous hat, which is only used as a shield when two Highlanders come to fisticuffs." Banter of this sort made the Tam o' Shanter disappear. He then donned a hideous shepherd's tartan cap, snouted "fore and aft," which was really more ugly than the other, so he was likewise soon chaffed out of wearing it. He finally appeared wearing a hard felt pot hat: " Ah, that's something decent! especially in a gale, when you are obliged to cram it tightly on your head; splendid cure for headaches!"

One afternoon Mr. P—— of Quebec made himself very objectionable to one of our youngest saloon passengers, without any warrant for it, so at the dance before referred to, a plot was suddenly arranged and carried into effect, which fairly " brought down the house." He was sitting watching the dancers with his hard pot hat on his knee, whilst my friend M—— had the chief stewardess for partner in a waltz. M—— weighs fifteen stone, and she, I should say, would turn the scale at thirteen stone. At the proper moment the ship *gave the required lurch*, and down flopped the fat stewardess in Mr. P——'s lap! His face was a study as he examined his hat, which now looked more like a concertina than an article of headgear. The applause and laughter that followed amongst those who were in the secret can be better imagined than described. M——'s health was afterwards drunk, and a special vote of thanks passed to him and his partner for their successful exploit. This was the first and only occasion on which I ever saw the slang phrase "sitting on a fellow" practically exemplified.

The temperature fell one day to 38° Fahr., very cold for the month of April, but the sea was on this occasion comparatively calm for the first time since we left Moville. The next morning, Sunday, we had lovely weather, the sun shining brightly, with not a cloud in the sky, and the deep blue water smooth as a mirror, just the sort of day for the last on board, to send you away with good impressions of the voyage, and to make you feel a kind of regret that it would soon be over.

Of course we had the usual "sweep" as to the number of the Pilot boat. When it first hove in sight it was just a little white speck on the horizon. Telescopes and field glasses were brought into requisition, and, after long staring and straining of our optics, the number, 9, was first of all faintly, then gradually more distinctly seen painted on the large mainsail. We slowed down as we approached our brother Jonathan, and soon we had our pilot and his portmanteau safely on board.

There are twenty-five of these pilot boats, each of them having sleeping accommodation for eighteen men. Of that number about six form the usual crew, and the remainder are pilots, who are dropped off one after another on to passing steamers bound for New York. They sometimes come out as far as 200 miles to meet incoming vessels, although the pilot is seldom asked to take command until Sandy Hook is reached, thirty-three miles from New York. We were 158 miles off when we took our pilot on board.

Service was again held in the saloon on the second Sunday of our voyage, but the sermon of Mr. H. K—— made most of us yawn. After dinner I was deputed to propose "The *Anchoria*, the Captain, Officers, and Crew." I said—"I supposed we must consider ourselves in American waters, and consequently would be bound by the customs of that country. As I had never been in America before, and couldn't possibly know whether after-dinner speeches were allowed there on Sunday, I hoped our American friends seated around the tables would forgive the breach of decorum, if there was any, in what I was doing," &c., &c. Capt. Campbell replied shortly, modestly, and gracefully. This gentleman has been a captain in the Anchor line for nearly thirty years, and he doesn't look fifty to-day. He is a strict disciplinarian, and at the same time a most genial fellow—a true gentleman and a kindly man, with always one or two good yarns to keep the dinner going merrily.

Everybody was astir at six next morning, even the " stowaway " appeared on deck carefully wrapped in a shawl in his mother's arms. The babe was kept out of sight, but the mother looked well and hearty.

CHAPTER II.

Arrival at New York—Passing the Customs—The Hotel Bus Trick—Rough Streets—Magnificent Buildings—Fire-escape Ladders—The Elevated Railroad.

THE sail into the harbour of New York is very pretty. Several islands are passed, and Bartholdi's huge statue of Liberty arrested our gaze a long way off. The peculiarly built tug boats, which at a distance looked exactly like large bottles standing in the water, and the immense ferry boats, some conveying railway trucks (or I should now rather say railroad freight cars), others transferring passengers, vehicles, and horses from New Jersey to New York, or New York to Brooklyn, passing and repassing, made it a lively scene. To the right a splendid view was had of Brooklyn Suspension Bridge, of which more by and by.

Meanwhile the steerage passengers had passed the doctor's inspection, and the Customs officers arrived on board. Before two of these officials we had all to appear in turn and sign a paper declaring the contents of our trunks, &c. As soon as we got into dock, and had our luggage put ashore, another officer was detailed off to compare our "declaration" with an actual examination of the contents of our boxes. If you have any goods with you not your own personal belongings, say, for instance, some material for a lady's dress, baby's dress, shoes, shawls, or gloves, it is always better to declare them, however insignificant in value they may be, because if you are taking them out as a present to friends you are not likely to be asked to pay any duty. At all events they let me off scot free.

We had been sufficiently warned about the extortionate fares demanded by the cabdrivers of New York, so we determined to go to our hotel, which was three miles off, by car or elevated railway; but first of all we tried to find the "Express"* man, in order to "express" our baggage there. We were not fortunate in our search inside the shed at the wharf, though we were assured he was about somewhere, and had just resolved that one of us should go outside to look for him, when a respectably dressed individual came up (he didn't touch his hat—you don't get much of that sort of thing in America) and addressed us, " Grand Union Hotel Bus, Sir?" "Yes, certainly, you are the man for us." Our luggage was placed on the roof, and we got inside of what appeared to be only a two-horse cab, but then we did not know what hotel buses were like in America. On arriving at our hotel, after a jolting over the worst paved streets it had ever been our lot to ride along, we discovered how completely we had been "taken in and done

* See page 112.

for." Five dollars was asked by our "bus driver," who was none other than an ordinary cabby of course, and five dollars *we had to pay.* I do think that in certain circumstances strong language is not only justifiable, but absolutely necessary as a safety valve for one's feelings! £1 0s. 10d. for a two-and-sixpenny ride! " Bang went a saxpence" indeed! The brother Scot who is credited with having used that expression should try New York next!

I have referred above to the state of the streets over which we drove to the hotel. A closer acquaintance with them in all parts of the city did not dispel the first bad impression we got. The stones look as if they had been thrown in anyway —no attempt having been made to get uniformity of size; some are two inches above others, and here and there mud holes are seen, showing that they have disappeared altogether. To make matters still worse the tramway rails are laid above the level of the causeway, somewhat on the principle of our railways, but not quite so high.*

On the other hand we never saw such magnificent blocks of business buildings anywhere. London's palaces and hotels and Houses of Parliament can hardly be surpassed, but there is a freshness about

* With the single exception of Washington, which is decently paved, not one city we visited in America—I exclude Canada—could boast of either a roadway or pavement that would compare favourably with the worst paved town we have seen in Scotland. New York, Philadelphia, and Baltimore are specially bad.

these piles of masonry in New York which makes them very attractive to a stranger just arrived from a provincial town in the old country. We were greatly astonished, however, at the incongruity of colour and design displayed everywhere. For instance we saw a nine-storey block built of red brick (very fine manufacture) adjoining a massive white marble building. A still more glaring example is to be found in the most fashionable quarter of the city—away far up Fifth Avenue, nearly opposite the palatial mansions of the Vanderbilts, where stands a beautiful stone-built church, sculptured and carved in the most elaborate fashion; and alongside is a small wooden carriage hiring establishment, then another small wooden shanty for selling candy sweets, and alongside that a wooden two-storey lager beer saloon.

Nearly opposite, I have already said, are the residences of the Vanderbilt family. There are three of these adjoining each other. One of them is so elegantly carved outside, with gilt frescoes, bronze railings, stone slabs for pavement of great dimensions—one stone we measured was 27 feet by 15 feet—and so luxuriously finished inside that it is said to have cost £1,000,000 sterling.

Ground is so very dear in New York most of the buildings are of great height; some of them tower aloft twelve or thirteen storeys. Nearly every business building, and all hotels and private stores, have one or more "lifts" or "elevators."

The great majority—certainly all the very high ones—have an outside iron stair, ascending in flights, zigzag fashion, from one window to another, to provide an escape in the event of a fire. In hotels, in addition to this iron ladder, there is generally a strong metal hook fixed inside each bedroom window, to which is attached a stout rope, long enough to reach to the ground, thus furnishing another safe means of escape, should it be impossible to reach the ladder in time of danger.

In New York the means of locomotion are ample. No city that I know of is better favoured in this respect. Tramways are laid in many streets double—two lines up and two down—and the elevated railways run in four lines from one end of the city to the other, all having their common terminus at The Battery.

The "elevated" attracts a stranger's attention in a striking manner, it appears so odd at first to see trains spinning along on rails laid on top of iron pillars erected in busy streets, but soon one gets accustomed to it. As a means of locomotion, for comfort, convenience, and cheapness, it surpasses anything we ever tried before. You ascend a stair from the pavement, pay five cents at the office, get a ticket, drop it into a box, which is in charge of a railway official, and you pass on to the platform, enter the train, and travel as far as you like. It is an admirable arrangement, for you have no more bother with your tickets, as there is only one class in the cars, and only one price, let your journey be long or short. Stations are situated every three or four blocks. A conductor stands on the platform of each car, and calls out the name of the station on approaching it. When the train starts again, he always shouts out where the next stop will be. The conductors are smart, respectable-looking men, but one and all of them have an unfortunate habit of pronouncing the names of the stations as indistinctly as possible. Every now and then we heard a remark of a passenger to his neighbour—" Did you hear what he said the next stop would be?" The reply invariably was—" No, sir, I didn't catch on."

In walking about town we frequently inquired of a policeman or any one passing the names of different buildings that arrested our attention. The information was always readily and politely given to us. In one case, however, we had evidently accosted a non-resident, for, on putting to him the usual question, he stopped, gazed intently at the building (his nether jaw working hard at a "quid" of tobacco all the time), expectorated, still keeping his eyes fixed on the object of our inquiry, and after a painful pause said, "I guess, stranger, I give it up," then turned on his heel and walked away. He appeared to think we had given him a rather difficult conundrum to answer! It was "so American you know."

CHAPTER III.

Hotels—Florists' Shops—All about Flats.

AMERICAN hotels are of two kinds— those conducted on the European plan and those on the American plan. Our experience, and that of every one we have met who has travelled any distance in the United States, compels me to unreservedly recommend the American plan. You pay four or five or more dollars a day, which includes everything, and get splendid fare for that. In the Grand Union Hotel,* New York, we paid one dollar a day for our bedroom, and took our meals where we chose, but we found this method a very expensive arrangement in comparison with our experiences elsewhere. A capital restaurant *à la carte* was "run" by the hotel, but prices were beyond reach altogether for a single individual to breakfast or dine alone when a variety of dishes was desired. We overcame this difficulty to some extent, and followed the usual custom in America, by ordering one dish for two and dividing. I give a few extracts from the Breakfast Bill of Fare—

* This hotel is conducted on the European plan—the charge for bedrooms only was one to three dollars—but in all other places we stayed in hotels which adopted the American plan.

HOTELS.

Two eggs, ...	20 cents.
One chop, ...	50 "
One steak, ...	60 "
One pot coffee and cream (two cups), . . .	25 "
Chicken's liver curried, .	40 "
Calves' brain—brown butter,	55 "
Cold corned beef, rump, .	30 "

The hotels all over the States are perfect models of what a hotel ought to be. The entrance hall is used almost like an exchange. You can come and go just as you please. You may walk in, write a letter, using the hotel notepaper, take possession of a rocking chair, smoke a cigar, spit all over the floor, and walk out again at your own convenience, without any one interfering with you. There is a barber's shop, druggist's store, telegraph office, railway ticket office, cigar and tobacco store, newspaper stall, and shoebrushing* and cloak-room all in or leading from the entrance hall. The hotel clerks are always at their desk, night and day in rotation, to take charge of guests' letters, which are placed in pigeon holes in alphabetical order as they arrive from the post, and are handed to the parties who inquire for them. The clerks also

---

* You have to pay to get your boots brushed, the charge varying from five to fifteen cents for a "boss shine." You must not put your boots outside your bedroom door at night to be cleaned for next morning, as is the custom in our country, or the chances would be against you ever seeing them again.

take charge of your bedroom key, and attend to the inquiries, wants, and complaints of all and sundry. The amount of general information they possess is extraordinary. Always to be found with a very polite manner and a dressy exterior, a pleasant fellow is the American hotel clerk. Whenever you are in a difficulty of any sort, apply to him and you will get good and reliable advice, if not absolute satisfaction.

Strawberries had been plentiful since the beginning of March—grown in the South—showing the variety of climate possessed by America. We got very fond of a delicious tit-bit called strawberry cake—a light sponge-cake covered with a layer of fresh strawberries, and switched cream on the top. Bananas — enormous luscious fellows, eight or ten inches long and one-and-a-half inch thick—were to be had very cheap, two or three for five cents. Hyacinths and pansies were blooming in abundance in the open air (this was early in April), and a feature worth noticing specially, was the great display of blossom in the florists' shops in Fifth Avenue and other fashionable streets up town. Immense hydrangeas covered with bloom, and all kinds of table and hothouse plants, were crowded on the floors of these shops, in the windows, and on the pavement outside. American millionaires can have very little difficulty in filling their houses with floral decorations when they give their grand entertainments.

We spent a very enjoyable evening in the house of one of our fellow-passengers in the *Anchoria*—Captain B. His wife is a granddaughter of Edmund Glover, and is a very charming and accomplished lady. She has travelled over a great portion of the globe with the captain, having roughed it not a little during some of their wanderings on the west coast of Africa, and other places of like nature. Their house is a top flat in Eighth Avenue, near Ninety-fifth Street, facing the Central Park.

I was anxious to find out all I could about the "flat" system in New York, so plied our kind hostess with questions bearing on it, which she most good-naturedly answered. I am also indebted for some of my information to an article which I read in *Cassell's Magazine*. Flats are not, I may say at once, much in favour in American cities any more than they are in England. In Scotland, as every Scotsman knows, they are much more in vogue. In a city like New York, however, where ground is so scarce and dear, the system is bound to extend and to come into favour amongst people who cannot afford to pay a fabulous price for a "lot" on which to build a cottage and "plant their own fig-tree." In Captain B.'s house there are five nice rooms, all leading directly into each other, with closets and pantries in plenty, also a comfortable, though not very roomy, bathroom. They give out all their washings, but many families who have adopted the "flat" system cling to their weekly wash, and instead of drying their clothes in the back green, which they have not got, they ascend a flight of stairs on to the roof, which is level, and there their poles and ropes are fixed up and the drying done as expeditiously, if not more so, than down below.

In New York the atmosphere is always remarkably clear, and not polluted by the foul smoke which we are so accustomed to in large towns in this country. Nothing but hard coal is burned, which gives off scarcely any smoke, and most houses are heated by steam or hot-air pipes, whilst gas stoves are largely used for cooking, so there is really no danger of the washing being soiled by "smuts," even though it be fluttering in the breeze high up amongst the chimney-pots. Water is laid all over the tenement, and a *chute* at the back of the house sends all ashes and refuse flying into a bin three storeys below, from whence the ashman removes them in the morning. The *chute* is probably only intended for kitchen refuse; nevertheless it refuses nothing offered to its amiable maw, and swallows old clothes and broken dishes as smilingly as ashes and potato skins. In the article above referred to, a story is told of a kitten disappearing down the *chute*, coming out all right at the ground floor, convincing those who witnessed the performance that pussy had not yet discovered an easy and proper passage to the feline paradise.

The coal cellar is on the lowest floor, and you have to bring up each day's supply yourself. With a speaking tube connected with the front door, every flat manages its own social and practicable business with the street, and from each flat the front door can be opened on the same principle as with us, by pulling up a brass knob connected with the door by a wire or chain.

The halls and staircases, which are all carpeted, are kept in order by a woman who comes twice a week; during the rest of the time they take care of themselves. A janitor or *concièrge* on the Parisian style would be a great improvement. A curious result of the want of a *concièrge* is shown in dealing with the postman for instance—I beg pardon, letter-carrier—there are no postmen in America. Three or four times a day a ring comes to the bell, a voice falls gently down the speaking tube into the ear at the lower end, which hears the simple airy interrogative "Yes?" Up from the regions down below comes the reply, "Letters." Thereupon the street door is pulled open, the letter-carrier enters, and stands at the foot of the staircase; a basket is let down with a long cord, and drawn up the next minute, containing the welcome or otherwise missives from the post.

Another time the bell rings. Expecting letters or a friendly call, down again goes the sweetlytubed "Yes?" Then from the regions of mystery below comes the pungent query—"Got any rags, papers, bottles?"

Some of these furnished flats have elevators, but there was none in the tenement where Captain B—— lived. In many cases no servants are kept—Sarah-Janes being a scarce and unsatisfactory commodity; but women can always be had at a dollar and a half per day to clean up and assist in rough work.

When Mrs. B—— had occasion to go out, she used to leave her card over the name-plate at the street door, with the word "out" written on it, so that friends and visitors might know when to ring up and when not.

CHAPTER IV.

Hoffmann House and Stewart's Luncheon Bars—Delmonico's—M——meets an Old Friend—Brooklyn Suspension Bridge—Produce Exchange—Eastman's—St. Patrick's Cathedral—Equitable Insurance Building—Barnum's Show.

WE visited many of the restaurants and luncheon bars, for which New York is justly famed. There can surely be nothing of their kind finer than the bars in Hoffmann House Hotel, and Stewart's, in Warren Street, off Broadway. In each of these places there are hung on the walls paintings almost priceless as works of art. One especially in Stewart's is worth noting. It is called "The Remains of the Hunt," and represents an old wooden door with heavy iron nails in it, and hanging thereon a hare, a pheasant, and some other things. The keyhole and the bolts—in fact the entire picture is painted with such rare fidelity to nature, that it took us some time to realize that we were only looking at a bit of canvas. In this bar there is also a painting of an old five-dollar note, and we could not positively tell whether it was a real one or not, without the aid of a magnifying glass. Ladies are requested by the proprietors of these valuable works of art to call before 11 a.m. if they desire to inspect them with comfort.

We also called at the world-famed Delmonico Restaurant, in Broadway, where the dudes and wealthy New Yorkers generally congregate on festive occasions. The cooking is said to be of the most *récherché* kind, but the charges are absurdly exorbitant in everything. For instance, for two " nips " of whisky we were charged forty cents, *i.e.* one shilling and eightpence per glass. The same quality and quantity of liquor could have been got in many good bars at exactly half this price.

At another restaurant not far off, we had an excellent dinner at a very reasonable figure—less than a dollar. During our meal M——, who was a sugar planter in the West Indies for twenty years, remarked to me that he could almost imagine himself back at the plantation, he felt so much at home amongst the negro waiters, who were hurrying to and fro carrying aloft above their heads trays which rested on the palms of their left hands turned back. After soup, our waiter addressed my friend by name, and inquired if he would " bring a bottle of beer, as usual." M—— looked hard at Sambo, and recognized him as one of his old Demerara coolies! How the poor fellow showed his ivories and grinned with delight when asked some questions about the old place familiar to both of them, and how grateful he was when M—— handed him a dollar on leaving! After such an accidental *rencontre*, we came to the conclusion that the world is not such a very big place after all.

I must now say something about the great Suspension Bridge which connects New York with Brooklyn. It is a most beautiful structure to look at, apart altogether from its merits as one of the greatest engineering triumphs of the century. Excepting the Forth Bridge, which is built on the cantilever as opposed to the suspension principle, it may be accurately described as the most wonderful bridge in the world. It is nearly one mile and a quarter in length, and stands 160 feet above high-water level. The centre track—about five or six yards wide—is exclusively for pedestrians, who each pay one cent as toll. On either side of this cable trains run back and forward between New York and Brooklyn, the fare for each passenger being only three cents. The outside tracks are for horse and carriage traffic—carriages being able to run two abreast on both tracks. The enumeration of these five tracks gives one a tolerable idea of the immense width and massiveness of this beautifully symmetrical structure. To an onlooker its size and proportions are hidden in its perfect symmetry.

On our way back from Brooklyn a poorly clad, half-starved looking man—it was quite an incident in itself to see such an unfortunate specimen of humanity in New York—stopped in front of two

Sisters of Mercy, raised his hat, and gave one of them a copper, which was gratefully accepted. Poor soul! he appeared to us to be more an object of charity than a dispenser of it.

Talking of poor men reminds me that we got a glimpse of the dregs of the society of New York in the district called The Bowery—rather a euphonious name for such a locality; but, generally speaking, we saw fewer evidences of squalor and dirt and poverty and misery than we were prepared to find in a city of its size and population.

Through the kindness of a gentleman, to whom we had a letter of introduction, we were admitted as honorary members of the Produce Exchange for one week. This Exchange, with its prototype in Chicago, of which I shall speak in its proper place, is admitted on all hands to be one of the biggest and most handsome of its kind, none better is to be found in any other city in the world. The ground floor is occupied chiefly by bankers and merchants' offices. The great hall or exchange proper is on the first floor, and here we alighted from one of the elevators, which are fixed up at all the different entrances to the building.

No description of the scene can convey to any reader an idea of the din and noise, which on our first entry nearly drove us crazy, as we mingled in the throng of excited brokers yelling out their prices for "future" or "spot," for wheat and corn. But we soon got familiar with our surroundings, and even the shouting appeared the most natural thing in the world under the circumstances. The floor was covered "thick as autumn leaves" with the remains of torn-up telegrams, letters, and contracts, mingled with grain, sawdust, and tobacco juice.

By again entering an elevator we reached the top of the large square tower which crowns the great edifice below. It stands 250 feet above the street level, and is familiarly known in business circles as the "Tower of Babel!" From here we got a really magnificent view of New York, New Jersey, and Brooklyn. Right below where we stood, on the other side of the river, a large passenger ferry steamer was on fire, ablaze from stem to stern. All the passengers got off in safety, but some poor horses on board had a narrow escape, being rescued after great trouble and danger to those engaged in the work of mercy.

Half an hour's ride on the "elevated" from the Produce Exchange took us to Fifty-ninth Street, where is situated the Eastman Packing Company's premises. Mr. Eastman received us very kindly, and personally conducted us over the works. He informed us they kill 500 cattle every day all the year round, except Sundays and holidays, and most of the meat is shipped to Liverpool and Glasgow. They also do a large business in canning, packing the meat into small tins and sending them over to Europe. Every bit of the animal is used up in one way or another, the bones and entrails even being carefully manipulated into some useful product. The process of making lard was very interesting, although a great drawback to watching the manufacture of this now much-used article of consumption was the horribly sickening smell which pervaded every chamber during its progress from the initial stage to the finish.

A short walk across several blocks brought us to the entrance gate of the Central Park, of which New Yorkers are so justly proud. We did little more than glance at it on this occasion, reserving an entire day for it on our return, so we strolled leisurely down Fifth Avenue and stopped to inspect St. Patrick's Cathedral.

This building has been twelve years in construction, and is not quite finished yet, although it is sufficiently advanced to admit of service being held inside. It is entirely composed of white marble, and has two spires about 150 feet high, most beautifully carved right up to the top. This is the handsomest church in America, and is admitted to be one of the finest *modern* cathedrals in the world.

Through the courtesy of Mr. H—— K—— of Wall Street we were introduced as honorary members of the Lawyers Club, a well-known institution. It has a suite of apartments, very luxuriously furnished, in the lofty Equitable Insurance Building. The reading and smoking rooms are marvels of comfort and convenience, whilst every possible luxury is provided for the members, including several handsomely fitted marble baths. We inspected, in the same building, the offices of the Equitable Insurance Company, which are well worth seeing. The grand staircase in the new City Chambers in Glasgow is the nearest approach to the style of the internal arrangements of this office that I can think of. Marble floors, marble counters, marble roof, marble walls, marble stairs—everything marble! The lavish outlay of money in this way must have been enormous.

We also visited Barnum's "Greatest Show on Earth;" but as Londoners have had an opportunity of seeing this big show, and unanimously passed a favourable verdict on it, I need not say more than that we thought we got too much value for our money. The attempt to watch four circuses with different performances going on in each at the same time was, to our way of thinking, more distracting than enjoyable.

CHAPTER V.

Cook's Tourist Tickets—Bogus Ticket Agents—Philadelphia—Easter Saturday—Washington—A Train Ferry—Locomotives—Railroad Cars—The Train Boy.

WE took tickets at Cook's for our tour, which was as follows:—Philadelphia, Baltimore, Washington, Cincinnati, Indianapolis, Niles, Kalamazoo, Chicago, back to Kalamazoo, Detroit, Windsor, Niagara, Toronto, Ottawa, Montreal, Plattsburg, Saratoga, Boston, Fall River, and steamer to New York. Cook's made up our bundle of tickets into a little book, and we had no trouble whatever afterwards.

There is a class of men in America who do a big "swindle" in railway tickets. They suddenly appear in a town, open a store, sell a number of tickets (which they say they have obtained in some extraordinary way) at a very reduced rate. Amongst them they throw in a few forged ones, and over and over again travellers discover, when too late, that they have been swindled. No doubt there are a great many respectable people who carry on business as ticket agents in every town; but a stranger never knows the correct one to go to, so undoubtedly the safest, and cheapest plan in

PHILADELPHIA.

the long run, is to go to a well-known firm like Cook's at the *beginning* of your tour, pay your money for the entire round, and see that you don't lose your tickets.

In going long journeys we took advantage of the Pullman or Wagner drawing-room car, or "sleeper" as they call it, by paying three to four dollars extra as required. For journeys of, say, the duration of half-a-day the ordinary car is quite as comfortable to travel in as any one could wish.

PHILADELPHIA is reached in about three or four hours by express train from New York. We had to cross by ferry to Jersey City, where we got on "board" the cars for the south. We landed in Philadelphia on Easter Saturday, and found the streets crowded, especially with young folks, white and black, laden with Easter toys, and evidently in thorough enjoyment of their holiday.

Some of the shops and stores in Chestnut Street, Walnut Street, and other central business streets that we strolled through, were very well worth seeing, and the immense warehouse of John Wannamaker, the Postmaster General of the United States, was pointed out to us. The streets are narrow compared with those of New York, but the buildings are a reasonable height, averaging two or three storeys. I believe there are about 800,000 inhabitants in Philadelphia, and the city covers nearly the largest area of any city in the States. We visited some of the principal buildings, and also got a glimpse of Fairmount Park—one of the largest and prettiest of parks belonging to any city in America.

Our stay at Philadelphia was spoiled to some extent by indisposition, which had overtaken me in New York the day before our departure southwards, and I did not feel sufficiently well to be able to see and do as much as under more favourable circumstances the importance of this large city demanded.

We reached WASHINGTON in a thunderstorm. The brilliant sheet lightning and tropical downpour reminded us that it is in the latitude of Gibraltar. Our luggage had been "checked"* through direct from New York, so we handed our brass tablet to the hotel porter, and in the evening had the happiness to see our boxes lying in our bedrooms all right. We made sure about getting into the right hotel bus this time, and all that we paid for a ride of about half an hour was 25 cents each, or one shilling.

On the way to Washington from Jersey City we had to cross a river about three quarters of a mile wide. The entire train, engine included, was run on to a great ferry boat—fully three hundred feet long—which carried us slowly across the stream. When it got moored at the dock on the opposite side, our engine shrieked with its whistle, tolled its big bell, and puffed away merrily on its

* See Railroad Check System, page 113.

journey. It was quite as exciting as it was a novel experience.

The locomotives are the most odd things to look at. Each has a lantern the size of the dial of an eight-day clock fixed in front of the funnel, and their foghorn whistle requires to be heard to be appreciated. Plenty of opportunities occur for the exercise of steam-power in this manner, as they are required to "toot, toot, toot" at all the level crossings, and to toll their heavy-toned bell to warn people to get out of the way! I shall have more to say about these level crossings further on, but meantime it is enough to observe that at nearly all of them a signal post is erected with the words "Beware of the Locomotive" printed thereon.

The railroad cars are very comfortable to travel in, and far in advance of our "pokey" boxes of railway carriages at home. They are similar to, though not so expensively furnished, as the drawing room cars on some of our railways here. There are generally three or four cars on every train, each one being about sixty feet in length, and passengers are allowed to walk from one end of the train to the other. They are heated in winter by means of steam pipes—steam being supplied from the engine, or else a stove is fitted up at one end, where frozen passengers may warm themselves. There is also a large stone jar containing water, with a block of pure ice in it, for drinking purposes, and lavatories are to be found in every car.

The conductor of the train holds a position similar to the captain of a ferry steamer. He walks all over the cars, takes the tickets, sits down beside you in the "smoker," joins you in a cigar, and commences a conversation with you. He is a superior class of man, take him all over, well educated, and possessed of a general fund of information, which is very useful to travellers. He is an agreeable fellow withal, and ladies, or others travelling alone, never fail to have a companion on the journey in the person of the genial conductor.

There is another individual on the cars peculiar to American railway travelling—I refer to what is called the "train boy," though the individual referred to is sometimes a man. He comes along the cars with travelling caps, papers, candy sweets, fruits, books, all in their turn, and plumps one packet on this "stranger's" lap and another on that. In a few minutes he returns, and if he sees you interested in the book which he had left in your care, he quickly closes it and recommends you strongly to buy it as a very exciting incident is recorded over the leaf where you were reading! A glib talker, an excellent salesman, a smart youth, is the train boy. He earns in wage and commission sometimes two or three dollars a day.

CHAPTER VI.

Washington — Description of the City — Office-seekers — Tobacco Chewers — White House — The Capitol — Niggers — An Immersion — Novel Advertising — John Chinaman — Baltimore — Canning Factories.

WASHINGTON is a charming city. The buildings are a reasonable size, and are either red brick relieved with sandstone and white marble, or white marble entirely. The streets are wide, and rows of pale green feathery-looking trees are planted in them all. Several of these avenues are a number of miles long (I am afraid to say how many), and in some cases the parks, which abound in this beautiful city, are merely continuations and extensions of the avenues.

The morning after the thunderstorm the air was like champagne, it was so light and clear. The same afternoon the thermometer read 80° in the shade, but still it was not uncomfortably warm.

In wandering through the streets it was difficult to realize that we were in an American city, one's conceptions of a place are sometimes so far wide of the mark. It is a town more like what one would expect to find in Southern Spain; but even Seville, with its cathedral and Tower of Gold, its Plaza Nueva, and palm trees, and Guadalquivir, was not more interesting to me than Washington, with its Capitol, and avenues, and Potomac.

The Ebbitt House, where we stayed, is one of the best hotels in Washington. It is conducted on the American plan, and, considering the splendid *menu* provided for guests, the well-cooked food, and the great variety of fruits, not forgetting a most comfortable bedroom, the charge of four dollars per day was very small.

The city was crowded with strangers and tourists during our stay, and our hotel was full of office-seekers, with their wives and daughters, from all parts of the States. These men were hanging on from day to day trying to secure some of the many appointments that were in the gift of the recently-elected President, and a weary wait and indifferent success must have been the lot of many of their number.

It was an interesting study to sit in the hall of the hotel and watch the different types of Yankee strutting up and down, chewing his tobacco or smoking his cigar, and squirting great puddles of tobacco juice all over the beautiful white marble floor. An old negro in uniform, with a curly grey woolly head and short beard, walked about drying it up with a mop as best he could. It shocked us exceedingly, especially when we saw any number of large spittoons scattered* all over the hall; but

---

* Spittoons are also always placed at intervals along passages and in bedrooms in hotels.

it is strictly accurate to say that they were evidently considered more for ornament than for use. Little wonder that there is always a separate entrance provided in hotels for ladies.

We visited the White House, the residence of the President—a very unpretentious abode for the ruler of such a vast country. The interior is moderately well furnished, but the blue drawing-room, where receptions are held, is a large and handsome apartment.

The Capitol stands on rising ground at the other end of the city, at the head of Pennsylvania Avenue. Built almost entirely of pure white marble, and surmounted by a dome nearly as high as that of St. Paul's Cathedral, it has a commanding appearance, and is an object of interest and beauty seen from miles around. The interior is used, as every one knows, as the meeting-place where the affairs of the Union are discussed in the Senate and in the House of Representatives. It contains also a large public library and some Government offices.

Beyond the Capitol we got on a tramcar to explore the suburbs in that direction. On reaching the terminus, we alighted and walked towards the Potomac. Great numbers of people were crossing the bridge to the other side of the river, so we followed the crowd, which had this peculiarity that nineteen out of twenty were niggers. At the other side an "immersion" was going on "from early morn till dewy eve." The papers next day stated that 248 negroes and negresses had been baptized and received into the Christian Church. They were overtaken in batches, but we only waited long enough to see forty, males and females, "dipped" by one of the Baptist clergymen. Dressed in pure white, standing in two rows, "shivering at the brink," one by one they were led into the water up to the waist by the minister, who dipped each in turn right over the head. It was a funny sight, though to those most concerned it must have been a very solemn one.

The banks of the river in the immediate neighbourhood were black with black people, singing negro hymns all the time. The Potomac, which is half a mile wide at this point, was covered with craft of every description, laden with inquisitive sightseers. The bridge on which we stood was crowded with people, and scores of vehicles were crossing and recrossing at a walking pace, conveying the converts and their friends to and from the scene of operations, the nigger-drivers flourishing their whips and singing, "I will fight for de Lor';" those seated behind taking up the refrain, "Yes, we will fight for de Lor'."

The fun amongst the darkies who were making helter-skelter for the banks was great. One nigger "gal" got on a few paces in front of her companions, one of whom shouted, "Look dar at ole mudder, she *ken* walk; dats cos she war at de country las' yeah." Banter of this innocent sort kept every one in the best of humour. The females were dressed in a manner which was, to say the least, striking. Green, blue, or red, with a yellow contrast, was the prevailing fashion. An enormous feather of startling hue was invariably fixed in their bonnet or hat, and even that peculiar article of feminine attire, which is difficult to describe, but which is said to resemble a bird-cage, was not awanting. We were much delighted with our romp amongst these nigger lads and lasses, they were so playful and happy and innocent in all the fun that went on.

A third of the inhabitants of Washington are black, and all the waiters and servants in the Ebbitt House Hotel are coloured. The negro makes a splendid waiter, and he must be endowed with a powerful memory to remember correctly the multifarious variety of dishes which the average American orders " all of a heap " for each meal. The Ebbitt House Hotel has an elegant dining-room, with white walls and white marble floor. Red tablecloths were always laid at supper time, 6 p.m., and they looked very pretty amidst their white and black surroundings. Supper in America means generally the same thing as a six o'clock dinner with us.

During one of our strolls through the city we came across a daring and novel style of advertising which, from its originality, is worth recording here. In the window of one of the finest shops in Pennsylvania Avenue was a wooden hencoop with turf laid around it, and some gravel and sand spread about. A hen was sitting inside the coop, meditatively contemplating her brood of twelve tiny little chicks, just out of their shells, running all over the window. This was the shopkeeper's method of conveying an "Easter Greeting" to all who passed that way, whilst a large poster intimated that Easter cards could be bought within very cheap.

In Washington there is a small colony of Chinese, most of whom earn a livelihood by doing laundry work. They get the credit of being very quiet inoffensive citizens, and rarely mix, except in the way of business, with anybody outside their own nationality.

Nothing but matters of pressing moment would tempt any tourist to stay overnight in Baltimore with lovely Washington so close at hand, so we paid our visit and arranged the business we had to attend to there by going up in the morning and returning at night. Express trains run at frequent intervals between the two cities every lawful day, the journey occupying a little less than an hour. At one part a considerable system of open drainage seems to prevail, which is anything but creditable to the municipality which allows it, or the inhabitants who tamely submit to such a primitive and malodorous state of affairs. The streets are as badly paved as Philadelphia or New York, but, nevertheless, it has all the appearance of being a thoroughly busy city. The chief industries are tobacco manufacturing, and the canning of fruits and vegetables, whilst a large business is also done in shipping.

We were privileged in being shown over some of the canning factories, the inspection of which we found both interesting and instructive. Oyster shells are so plentiful—the oyster beds being in Chesapeake Bay—that some roads and wharves are made entirely with them. When well consolidated they form a road which is very pleasant and noiseless to drive along.

On our return to Washington we paid a visit to Auerbach's Opera House, and spent three pleasant hours listening to a remarkably tuneful opera, written by an American, entitled the "Pearl of Pekin." One of the actors gave a most lifelike imitation of a Chinaman, but we were so favourably impressed with the clever acting and singing of all the members of the company that it is hardly fair to particularise. Altogether our stay at Washington had been a most delightful one, and it was with feelings of sincere regret that we could not prolong our visit beyond the time originally fixed for our departure. The events immediately following are reserved for another chapter.

CHAPTER VII.

Start for Cincinnati—The Potomac—Alleghany Mountains—
Cumberland—Dining on the Cars—Cincinnati.

OUR journey westwards to Cincinnati was made in the St. Louis express of the Baltimore and Ohio R. R. Company. Shortly after leaving Washington we entered a very mountainous country, the railway track following closely the windings of the river Potomac, and gradually ascending towards its source in the Alleghany Mountains. The scenery was extremely picturesque, but the travelling very rough owing to frequent curves and gradients. Several of our fellow passengers turned sick with the shaking, but probably the overheated car had also something to do with this result.

One very interesting town, Cumberland, at which we made a halt for twenty minutes, called forth our admiration as being the prettiest place, from its situation, we had yet seen on our travels in America. It lies nestled in hills, whilst tree and river lend it a peculiar charm, which can only be appreciated by one who has seen some of our pretty hamlets in the Highlands of Scotland.

A rare specimen of American ingenuity was

presented to our gaze at this place. A gentleman was enjoying his afternoon ride on a tricycle, and in a neat basket arrangement fitted up in front of the machine was comfortably fixed a bright little two year old boy, who seemed to enjoy the ride as well as his father.

At 10 p.m. our Pullman drawing-room car was transformed into a sleeping carriage, and "all aboord"* were soon under the blankets. At 7.30 next morning we had to get up, and the car again resumed its drawing-room appearance for the rest of the day.

All sorts of meals were served on the train at the shortest notice. Breakfast, dinner, and supper were ready at certain hours; and when we felt inclined for something to eat, an ingenious table contrivance was fixed up where we sat, and tea, coffee, soups, *entrées*, or joints, served piping hot, almost as soon as ordered, and quite as good as could be got in a hotel.

CINCINNATI was reached after a journey of eighteen hours. It is a city of about 500,000 inhabitants, and resembles Glasgow in many respects, such as its river and warehouses, but more particularly in the colour of its atmosphere, which is very smoky.

My travelling companion's nephew, a bright young lad of sixteen, acted as our *cicerone*. He

---

* The conductors always shout "All aboord" before the train moves out of a station, see p. 51.

took us everywhere by tramcar and otherwise; but with the exception of the suburbs, which are really lovely, the Cincinnatonians being very proud of them, there was nothing whatever of interest to be seen from the point of view of a tourist. The General Post Office is a massive granite building (a prominent feature in many American cities is the Post Office), and the suspension bridge across the Ohio is a handsome structure half a mile long, and stands 170 feet above high-water level. It connects Cincinnati with Covington.

The Ohio is a very shallow stream, notwithstanding its hundreds of miles of length, so the steamers are all of light draught, flat bottomed, and stern-wheelers, like those in use on the Nile. They have all three decks, and most of them have two funnels. The paddle steamers we saw at New York are of quite a different build, the paddles being at the usual place at the sides, and they have the "walking beam" on the upper deck, which is not the case with the Ohio boats.

CHAPTER VIII.

Indianapolis—Niles—Kalamazoo—Newspaper Gossip—Some boastful Americans—"The finest in the World; Yes, Sir"—Railway Stations—Level Crossings.

LEAVING Cincinnati at 8.20 a.m., after two days' stay, we reached Kalamazoo at 10.30 p.m. same evening—a long dusty and most uninteresting journey through country as flat as Lincolnshire all the way. We travelled by the Cincinnati, Wabash, and Michigan R.R. This route takes the traveller by Indianapolis, Wabash, Goschen, Elkhart, and Niles, and we had to change cars at the first and also the last mentioned of these places.

At NILES, Michigan, there was a wait of an hour, so those going in the direction of Kalamazoo and east had a good opportunity of seeing all that was of interest in this pretty little town. It was like an oasis in the desert, after the journey we had had so far. A river, fifty yards wide, and well wooded on both banks, divides it in two; and three neat if not very substantial bridges are thrown across the stream, which afford ample communication and access to all parts of the town.

Two hours' journey from Niles and we arrived at KALAMAZOO, still in the State of Michigan, a town of 10,000 inhabitants. It also is situated on a river, and is an equally beautiful place. The name is of either Indian or Dutch origin, and signifies "boiling caldron." A great many acres of marshy land lie round it; and a large industry is the cultivation of celery, in which a considerable number of Hollanders or Dutch, or descendants of Dutch families who settled there early in the century, are employed. The main street, Michigan Avenue, and the upper end of Burdick Street, have quite a busy look for such a small place.

Kalamazoo is a junction of several railroads which intersect the State of Michigan, so the farming population for many miles round have easy access to it to do their marketing. The business part of the town is nearly all built of brick, and some private residences are similarly built, but the greater portion of them are of wooden construction. The villas are nearly all painted white, with green venetian shutters; and in summer evenings whole families are to be seen sitting out in the verandah, without which no residence having any pretension to comfort is complete. Trees grow luxuriantly, the "sidewalks" being nearly all between two rows, and thus many streets have four lines of trees right down from end to end. The town is lighted by electricity, the effect of which amongst so much foliage is very beautiful indeed.

Every city in America appears to have some speciality which its inhabitants boast about. I was seriously asked by a native of Kalamazoo if I did not think it the prettiest place in America! Not having been everywhere in that vast country, of course it was impossible to give a definite answer, but I had to admit that it was one of the prettiest towns we had as yet visited during our wanderings.

The next day the *Kalamazoo Gazette* had a short paragraph in its first column, which I give here, hoping it will amuse the reader as much as it amused me. It was to the following effect:— "Mr. Archibald Porteous, of Glasgow, Scotland, who is on a tour in America, and is at present visiting his brother, whom he hasn't seen for forty years (*sic*), is said to have expressed the opinion that Washington and Kalamazoo are the two most beautiful cities on this continent." This must have been very interesting news to the vast majority of the citizens of Kalamazoo, who, with the exception of perhaps a dozen of them, never heard of me before! Besides, I am fortunately still on the sunny side of forty, and so is my brother, so the absurdity of the whole paragraph is apparent. Gossip of this sort bulks largely amongst news in all American papers.

If the citizen of Kalamazoo boasts of his town in its entirety, the New Yorker, with more cosmopolitan ideas, is content to speak triumphantly of a part. He points with the finger of pride to the Suspension Bridge, and with good reason; but when he tells you that St. Patrick's Cathedral, in Fifth Avenue, is "the finest in the world; yes, sir!" don't believe him! It goes without saying that New Yorkers who have "done the round trip" to Europe, do not commit themselves in this absurd way.

Then a Baltimore man will tell you they have the "finest park in America; yes, sir;" a Philadelphian will tell you the same about his city; the Cincinnatonian proudly asserts they have the finest cemetery of any city in the States, and the man from Indianapolis (in this instance the conductor of the train on which we travelled from Cincinnati) told us just as we were entering his native city that we were steaming into "the finest railroad depôt in the world; yes, sir!" The Buchanan Street Station, Glasgow, of the Caledonian Railway, and the Princes Street Station, Edinburgh, of the same Company, are two of the worst railway stations, considering the importance of the cities in which they are located, that I know of in Scotland, but neither of them is much inferior to that of Indianapolis; so that the reader can judge of our surprise and disappointment when we alighted from the train and looked around us in the "finest railroad depôt in the world!" The building containing the offices in connection with the station was good enough in its way, but even it in no sense deserved the exaggerated encomium of our friend the conductor.

The railway stations in America are mostly very unpretending structures.* In country districts they are mere wooden sheds, but in towns like Philadelphia, Baltimore, and even Kalamazoo, they are very comfortably fitted up with convenient waiting-rooms, which have every appliance in the shape of stoves and hot-air or steam-pipes for heating in winter, and fanners for keeping them cool in summer. The depôts consist of waiting-hall, booking-offices, baggage-room, and newspaper stalls, but there are no platforms as with us; the tracks are simply planked between the metals, and you have sometimes to cross several lines of rails to get to the train you wish to travel by.

The train starts at the advertised time without any warning; no guard's whistle or any signal whatever. The guard, or conductor as he is called, simply cries "All aboord!" and off you go, the engine tolling its bell to warn people in front to get out of the way.

In a new country like America many towns had their beginning before the railways that now run through them were made, and, as a consequence, the number of level, or grade, crossings that one sees everywhere simply takes one's breath away. That these are a great source of danger is evident

---

* The Station of the New York Central R.R. in New York is a splendid pile of buildings, and is the best we saw in America.

from the number of accidents which are daily chronicled in the newspapers. We had not yet seen a railway bridge, except over a stream, and these for the most part were very rickety wooden structures, across which all trains are compelled to run at a very reduced rate of speed. In Kalamazoo there are at least thirty level crossings within a mile of the Post Office. Trains run across the main streets of the town; tramway lines and roads and footpaths all being intersected at random by railroads. In many places there is no protection whatever, by gate or otherwise. The only warning you get of the approach of a train is the engine "tooting," and tolling its bell; but in country districts this precautionary measure is often neglected, and frequently appalling consequences ensue.

Within a week of our visit to Kalamazoo two accidents occurred. In one case a train ran into a "buggy," or light dogcart, in which were seated two young ladies, who fortunately escaped with only broken limbs; the horse was killed outright and the "buggy" smashed into matchwood. In the other a train ran into a tramcar in the centre of the business portion of the town, and killed six ladies instantaneously, and seriously injured several other passengers. Shortly after this the newspapers chronicled a similar catastrophe in Chicago. A train, crossing one of the streets there, ran with terrific force, considering the locality it was in, into a funeral *cortége*, killing the driver and all the occupants of the coach immediately following the hearse.

I believe the legislative assembly of Albany has just passed a bill providing for the total abolition of all grade crossings in their State within the next twenty years. No doubt similar action will be taken in many other States, but an effort cannot be made too soon to endeavour to remove a danger which has been allowed to exist too long. The evil has grown to such an extent without any serious attempt having been made to grapple with it, that I do not hesitate to characterize it as a disgrace to a civilized nation.

CHAPTER IX.

Kalamazoo—Americans and British Politics—The Irish Question—Presbyterian Church Service — Galesburg — Richland — Windmill Water Pumps.

THE Americans we met here were just what we found them in other places, kind and hospitable to a degree, with no fuss about it. One very praiseworthy feature about them all is that they are, each and every one, immensely proud of their country.

Considering the interest they are supposed to take in the politics of Great Britain, we were amazed to find how little the average American really does know of this subject. For instance, many with whom we had the pleasure of conversing seemed to think that Ireland is being treated by Britain in a fashion similar to what Poland was by Russia some years ago. This is explained to some extent by the fact that their information is entirely derived from a one-sided source, the reports that are cabled out as news from here being highly spiced accounts of evictions, suspensions of Irish members, and things of that sort, *and nothing else*. All this is done by interested persons at this side, partly for the benefit of politicians over there who angle for the Irish vote, but chiefly to keep alive the fiction about "the poor distressed downtrodden country" amongst the dollar senders, who are the bones and sinew, the life and breath of the agitation in Ireland.

Now Americans, if they are anything, are matter-of-fact and practical. Those with whom we conversed only knew about Ireland, as already stated, from Home Rule or Fenian sources. They had little or no knowledge of the beneficent land laws which had been passed in recent years for the benefit of the farmers in Ireland; of the land courts where tenants can have their rents revised and fixed, independent of the landlord altogether; of the extreme licence extended to the Irish national newspaper press, in the amount of personal abuse it is allowed to heap with impunity on the members of the British Government, and other matters of a like nature. We explained that when this same press writes scurrilous articles about some obscure individual, whose only crime is, perhaps, that he has been honest enough to pay his rent, and holds him up to scorn, suggesting boycotting and intimidation, then in that case the cowardly hand that has directed the cruel blow which is certain to fall on the humble peasant, is grasped by the hand of the law, and justice generally decrees a certain term of imprisonment on the culprit, and rightly too.

When we had satisfied their curiosity in respect

to these questions, they generally gave vent to the opinion that there must be an amount of bunkum and humbug and sham about the supposed grievances of Ireland which they never dreamt of, and that Americans would find means of solving the Irish problem in a different and more speedy and drastic manner than we Britishers would ever think of doing.

We were all agreed as to the misgovernment of Ireland in the past, but with so many evidences before them of the desire of Great Britain now to do justly between man and man, to protect the law-abiding citizen from the village ruffian, to enforce the law and punish the law-breaker, and at same time steadily to keep in view the removal of every grievance, it seemed to our American friends the most childish behaviour on the part of Irish politicians to keep alive an agitation which, if successful, would undoubtedly not bring any material benefit to Ireland, *however much it might confer on themselves*, and would assuredly lower the *prestige* of Great Britain in the eyes of the civilized world.

Americans see far enough ahead to know that those who pay the piper consider they have a right to select the tune, and they said that nothing but the independence of Ireland would ever satisfy the aspirations of Irish Americans, no matter what Irish members of Parliament might say on platforms at home. So much, then, for the supposed sympathy of Americans with the Home Rule movement! I believe I am within the mark in stating that the only *real* friends in America of the Nationalist party of Ireland are the inveterate haters of Britain, and the only inveterate haters of Britain there are the members of the Clan-na-Gael and kindred murderous societies.

Some esteemed Gladstonian friends of mine will probably not have found the foregoing particularly pleasant reading. But this being a personal narrative, I am bound, at the risk of giving offence, to place on record my impressions truthfully and faithfully. I recommend them therefore to study the Irish question in America first, before committing themselves further to a policy which will certainly lead them they know not whither.

On the first Sunday of our week's visit to Kalamazoo we attended service in the Presbyterian Church, of which Professor Loba is minister. The preacher's desk stood in the centre of a platform which was literally a mass of hydrangeas in full bloom. The service began by the whole congregation standing up, immediately after the voluntary was finished, and singing, without previous intimation from the pulpit, " Praise God, from whom all blessings flow." The rest of the service followed pretty closely that in use in Presbyterian churches at home, with the exception that an anthem was sung by the choir before the sermon, as is the custom in the Church of England.

One day we went by train to GALESBURG, about sixteen miles north of Kalamazoo, where Mr. A. O——, a wealthy farmer and a distant relative of the writer's, met us with a waggonette and pair and drove us to his farm, about five miles from the station. Mr. O. owns a tract of land of about 200 acres, all under cultivation. The dwelling-house and outhouses are well fitted up, all wooden built, but very solid-looking structures.

Later on the same day we drove to Mr. I. P.'s farm at RICHLAND, where we received an equally hearty welcome. Mr. P—— goes in more for rearing stock than for crop raising. He has a fine breed of horses, and his cattle, sheep, and pigs were wandering about by the score. The pigs are allowed to roam through the fields with the sheep and cattle, feeding chiefly on roots or anything edible they can pick up. What a difference from the condition of their brother "piggies" in the Old Country, where they are penned in a "stye," often standing up to their girths in filth! The fields are not marked off by hedges or dykes, but chiefly by what are known as snake fences—a series of thin logs laid on top of each other in zigzag fashion. Here and there wire fences are to be seen, but they are the exception.

In this part of the country streams and rivers are scarce, consequently farmers are obliged to bore for water. Sometimes they have to get down sixty feet to reach it, and when found they insert a pipe and erect a pump, on the top of which they fix a windmill. By this means the pumps are constantly working, and the tanks always kept full for horses and cattle to drink from. We saw some fish the size of fair average trout swimming in one of the drinking troughs, this being the best aquarium available to the youthful and enterprising pisciculturist who placed them there at first.

The sheep were a more diminutive species than what we generally see in this country, and wool grows thickly on their face from the eyebrows upwards, which gives them a strange look.

The return journey to Kalamazoo was made by road, Mr. P. driving us home in a waggonette drawn by a pair of "spanking trotters," a breed of horses which Americans go in largely for, and are widely interested in. Trotting matches are as popular in America as race meetings and steeplechases are with us.

CHAPTER X.

Chicago—Buildings—Train Tramcars—The Seven Sisters Grand Pacific and Palmer House Hotels—Walking on Silver Dollars—Board of Trade—Old Hutch—The Leland House—Hustlers—Lincoln Park—The Stockyards.

FIVE hours in the express over the Michigan Central R.R. brought us to CHICAGO, the "empire city of the west." A cooking car and a dining car were attached to the train, and for one dollar a very good dinner was served up to us *en route*. This line, being a continuation of the New York Central, is mainly owned by the Vanderbilts, and is a most comfortable one to travel over. I should say it is one of the few solid railroad tracks of America.

Several interesting towns are passed on the journey, notably Pullman, which derives its name from the inventor of the Pullman car, and which is almost solely inhabited by the workmen and their families connected with the immense factory where these luxurious travelling conveyances are made.

If my remarks with reference to the buildings of New York were reproduced here they would express, with tolerable accuracy, what our impressions were of Chicago, only "more so." I fancy there are several blocks in Chicago which, for height and massiveness and daring of design, eclipse anything of a like nature in New York, or anywhere else for that matter. The Auditorium Building, the Board of Trade or Produce Exchange, and the Post Office would be a credit to any city, and there are a number of business blocks, without specifying any one in particular, that might be included in the same category.

Elevators are as much in use here as in New York; you hardly ever require to climb a weary flight of stairs to reach an office, as lifts are fitted up in nearly all the principal buildings and business premises.

There are as yet no elevated railroads, though the proposal has been mooted; but the tramcars, which have no outside seats as with us, are mostly worked by cable. Three or four cable cars are sometimes joined together, and they travel at considerable speed all over the city just like trains, an interval of a couple of minutes or so intervening between each set and those following. They only stop at certain cross streets, and run on the right-hand set of rails in the direction they are going, instead of on the left, as with us. In driving, and all kinds of locomotion, the rule of the road in America is exactly the reverse of the custom of our country.

In summer open cars are used, with a framework of iron, over which an awning is fixed as a shelter from the sun. Sometimes, however, the roof is of wood, and you enter and leave at the sides, after the fashion of the workmen cars which are in use in Glasgow. Passengers are allowed to travel on the front and rear platforms of the ordinary winter cars.

As in Washington, so here we saw another daring style of advertising, during one of our perambulations through the city. Six tall women, dressed in white, were standing in the windows of a store, combing out their hair, which hung in every case in abundant profusion from their heads to their feet. Inside they sold a " Wonderful Hair Restorer." Bills at the door invited passers by to " walk in, nothing to pay;" so in we went, and found about a score of people listening to a lady glibly discoursing on the merits of the wonderful lotion.

The " Grand Pacific " and the " Palmer House " are two of the largest and finest hotels in America, and visitors to Chicago should not fail to see them, they are fitted up and finished in such elaborate style. The barber's saloon in connection with the Palmer House is the most luxurious place of the kind we ever saw, and no idea can be formed of the lavishness displayed in all directions, as even the floor is beautifully inlaid with tiles and *real silver dollar pieces.* Five or six hundred of these latter are cemented in the floor at regular intervals of about twelve inches apart, and the effect is very pretty. Verily "almighty dollars" must be plentiful with some people when they can afford to make pavements with them!

Through the kindness and courtesy of Mr. M. C. L——, to whom I had a letter of introduction, we were admitted members of the Board of Trade ("the finest Exchange in the world; yes, sir") during our sojourn in the city, and it was intensely interesting to watch the members of the "wheat ring" yelling—no other word will describe it—at each other over their transactions.

One old man, Mr. Hutchison (he looked nearly seventy), was pointed out to us as being one of the millionaires of America, his fortune having been made in wheat speculations. In the summer of 1888 he it was who effected the great wheat "corner," which was the general topic of conversation on this side of the Atlantic as well as the other at the time, and thereby netted for his own pocket 2,000,000 dollars in about a couple of months. When we entered the Exchange on our first visit, he was seated on a cane chair rocking quietly to and fro on its hind legs, with his back to the wheat ring, watching the prices as indicated by the clock-like apparatus suspended on the gallery in front of him. This is worked by the presiding clerk of the ring, who registers every transaction that takes place by means of a telegraph on his desk communicating with the indicator before mentioned.

Mr. Hutchison wore a shady soft knock-about hat, Gladstone collar, black tie, grey flannel shirt, open waistcoat, and greenish-black Oxford coat, with trousers of the same material, and he looked the most disinterested man in the hall.

When the indicator touched a certain point, prices having fallen a half per cent. during the time we were watching him, up he jumped off his chair, elbowed his way through the crowded ring like a youth of twenty, and left a card on a small table which stood in the centre, then made his way quietly back to his old seat. We were informed that he had laid his card down and probably told everybody to enter all they cared to sell *at a price*, and he would buy the lot. After a lull, prices again came back a quarter per cent., but he looked perfectly indifferent, not a muscle moved on his exquisitely mobile face, and every one who approached to speak to him was received with perfect *nonchalance* and the blandest smile. No one knew, not even himself, how many thousands he had at stake that morning, but there he sat as expressionless as a sphinx, and, so far as his intentions were concerned, quite as uncommunicative. A strange, tough old man! They call him Old Hutch, the Wheat King!

Dining at the Leland House was a luxury: splendid bill of fare, and a capital orchestra played all the time the meal was in progress. We had the pleasure of entertaining some friends whom we used to know in Scotland, now settled in Chicago. One, Mr. T——, who was in the tea trade in Edinburgh, went to Chicago about ten years ago to fight his way, and is now one of the "boss" tea brokers there. The active, pushing business men are called "hustlers," and Mr. T—— has well earned this designation.

On a warm sunny afternoon during our stay we took a drive by way of Lake Front to Lincoln Park, passing on our way thither the mansion of Mr. Robert Lincoln, at present American minister to the Court of St. James'. It is a handsomely laid out park, though not large. A part of it reminded us of one of our own seaside resorts, for there were any number of little boys and girls in charge of their nursemaids making castles and sand-pies on the shore of Lake Michigan, whose seemingly boundless expanse stretched away to the horizon. These great inland seas of America are in reality oceans, and the cities on their shores great seaports. The shipping of the port of Chicago almost equals in tonnage the aggregate of that of New York. Vessels leaving Chicago for certain ports are sometimes out of sight of land for days at a time. How small our little lakelets in the Old Country appear in comparison!

No stranger visiting Chicago ever thinks of leaving without seeing the stockyards, which are situated in the south-western portion of the city, and are reached by train and tramcar. Railroad cars with their living freight are run from all parts of the country right into the middle of these immense slaughter-houses, so that the extensive cattle ranches of the west and the great beef-distributing centre of America are in direct contact with each other. To see the stockyards properly in one day it would be necessary to "do" them on horseback, they cover such an immense area of ground, and are divided into lots belonging to different dealers. Swift & Co.; Armour & Co.; Libby, M'Neil, & Libby; and Fairbank are the principal proprietors. All these firms do a big business in America, and also in Europe, in raw beef, canned meats, and hams. In the one establishment we visited 2500 head of cattle and 5000 pigs are slaughtered daily. In some cases the cattle are shot, some felled by hammer, some killed with the knife. They are placed in enclosures, so many at a time, and are gradually driven from one barrier to another until they reach the last of all, where they are despatched. They are then drawn through a sliding door into a great hall reeking with blood, where hundreds of carcases of newly killed animals are being prepared for the markets by some hundreds of men. The sight is a sickening one, and not worth seeing twice.

Pigs are penned in a similar manner to the cattle, and when they in turn reach the condemned

CHICAGO, THE STOCKYARDS.

cell a couple of active attendants quickly affix a noose round one of their hind legs, and in an instant machinery swings them aloft amidst most heartrending squeals. They are now carried along in this manner a couple of yards, where is posted the killer, who stands here all day long (except of course at meal hours) doing nothing else save plunging his long knife into each poor brute's throat as it passes by. On they go a little farther, where a halt of nearly a minute is made to allow them to bleed freely, then, one by one, the machine automatically drops them into a vat of hot water, many reaching this stage only half dead. When sufficiently scalded they are turned over by two men with long poles into a sieve, which raises each one in turn on to a table, where another attendant stands affixing a hook to their nose, and they are dragged along, still by machinery, through a rotary brush, which completely strips their hair off. They are then once more swung aloft by the hind legs, and in this manner onwards they glide in a continuous stream, passing twenty or thirty men, each stationed at his post with one particular duty to perform, and in less than ten minutes from the commencement of his journey to paradise poor piggy is into halves and quarters, and laid in the ice chamber to be cooled, salted, and packed, ready to supply the markets of the world.

CHAPTER XI.

Departure from Chicago—Arrival at Detroit—City Hall—Woodward Avenue—Windsor—Steamer on Fire—"Finest Fire Brigade in the World; Yes, Sir!"—Policemen, &c.

HE return journey to Kalamazoo was made in the company of many American tourists who were bound for Europe. There were also some disappointed Oklahoma "boomers" in the train, gladly retracing their steps eastwards and homewards, after discovering that Oklahoma was not the Utopia they had fondly imagined it to be before its absorption into the Union.

A quiet Sunday was spent at Kalamazoo with my brother, Dr. J. W. F——, and other friends, whose kindness and hospitality had been unbounded, and the next day we started for DETROIT, a journey of a little over four hours from Kalamazoo.

The weather had been recently very hot, about 85° in the shade, but all the time of our stay in Detroit a nice cool breeze blew from the river, which made it possible to do our sight-seeing with some comfort.

Detroit is a very beautiful city, with many fine buildings, broad streets, and long pretty avenues.

From the top of the tower of the City Hall we got a splendid view of the town and surrounding district, and across the river to Windsor, in Canada.

We had a letter of introduction to Mr. S——, a Glasgow man, who arrived in Detroit in 1872, with more determination and courage and *grit* in his composition than money in his pocket, but who is now, owing to his industry and perseverance, one of the "bosses" of a furniture store in Woodward Avenue as big as Wylie & Lochhead's in Buchanan Street, Glasgow. Mr. S—— was kind enough to hire a carriage-and-pair, and we spent half-a-day driving leisurely all round the city, he pointing out the various features of interest. We pulled up for a little while at his house, a handsome villa off Woodward Avenue, where we had the pleasure of making the acquaintance of his wife and family.

An old Edinburgh friend, Mr. A. S——, joined us by appointment in the evening, and conducted us to the wharf, where we got on board the ferry steamer which plies between Detroit and Windsor. We landed at the latter place, and walked through some of the streets. The difference in the outward signs of wealth and prosperity between the two towns was very striking—Detroit, a flourishing, busy, increasing centre of industry and manufactures; Windsor, only one mile off, a backward, sleepy, and most uninteresting townlet. "How is this?" we asked. Some Americans replied it was the government, others said "it was the difference in the people;" but whatever the cause, the distinction was most marked, and I leave it to some one else to supply a reasonable explanation. Speaking for M—— and myself, our feelings were very mixed indeed, as we wandered through the streets of Windsor.

We had just returned to Detroit, and were comfortably seated at the door of our hotel enjoying a cigar, when a blaze of fire shot up to the sky at the river side about fifty yards off. A large shed intercepted our view, but we surmised that a steamer was in flames, and in this we were correct. Five or six steam fire-engines were on the spot in two or three minutes, and in half-an-hour they got the fire under control, but not until a large part of the vessel was destroyed.

What a place for tornadoes and floods and fires America is! The country is so extensive that there is always some startling event happening in some part of it. We certainly had a large enough experience of fires to last us for a long time. During our stay in New York there was a 5,000,000 dollars blaze, also a river steamer burnt, and several minor conflagrations. While we were in Cincinnati a pork factory, value 2,000,000 dollars, was completely gutted, nothing but the blackened walls remaining. While in Chicago a dry-goods store, value 1,000,000 dollars, and a theatre were burnt. In Kalamazoo one of the railway stations was partly destroyed from the same cause; and here again in Detroit the same thing.

The fire department in Detroit is said to be " the most perfect in the world; yes, sir," and in this instance for once we were disinclined to dispute the claim. About half-a-dozen engines arrived on the scene almost simultaneously with the alarm of the outbreak being given, and they got to work in the most rapid and business-like manner. The water-cocks having been in first-rate working order, no delay was caused on their account, as is sometimes the case in old-fashioned towns in our country, and the copious supply of water soon subdued the flames. Part of the duties performed by the fire department is the regular examination of the water-cocks all over the city—a very important matter, and I fear one that does not receive the attention it merits in many towns in this country. How often one reads in the papers at home, "that the fire brigade arrived quickly on the scene, but some delay was caused owing to scarcity of water," or "the water-cock was rusty, not having been used for so many years, and some time elapsed before the hose was attached," &c. Readers of our newspapers will see cases of which the above are samples recorded every day. In all respects, therefore, the Detroit fire department is as nearly perfect as a fire department could be, and is a worthy example for every city in the universe to follow.

Making these remarks about the fire brigade at once suggests a passing reference to the police force here; and what refers to them is applicable also to all their brother "bobbies" in the different cities we visited. For the most part they are smart men, polite to strangers, and military-like when on duty. They wear a light-grey tweed uniform, cut in something like the shape of the clothing of our own members of "the force," and in addition they wear a stand-up linen collar and a scarf, which gives them quite a masher appearance. They are well paid—in New York, at any rate, they get 800 to 1000 dollars a-year.

The tramway guards, or tramcar conductors, as they are called, are also a superior class of men, and all wear a uniform. They earn from 500 to 600 dollars a-year; but food and clothing are so much dearer in America compared with Great Britain, that their condition is not greatly better than that of their brethren in this country.

CHAPTER XII.

Departure from Detroit—Arrival at Niagara—The Falls—Whirlpool—Advice to Visitors.

WE travelled by the Grand Trunk Railway of Canada from Detroit to NIAGARA, a journey of seven hours—in our case a very hot, dusty one—through flat uninteresting country. Shortly after leaving Detroit we were transported across the river to Windsor in one of the train ferry boats, which I have already described. The land alongside the route of the railway is nearly all parcelled out to small farmers, who are gradually clearing the forest, and cultivating the soil. This whole region appears to have been at one time a dense forest. After the trees are sawn through and felled, the stumps left in the ground are burnt, and decay does the rest to clear the way for the plough.

From Windsor to Clifton, where we left the train, the railway runs through Canada. At Clifton it crosses the railway bridge which spans the river Niagara, and re-enters American territory.

We were advised to go to Clifton House Hotel, on the Canadian side, which is romantically situated close to the cliff overlooking the Horse-shoe

Fall. It was two miles from Clifton Station, so we made a reasonable offer of one dollar fifty cents, or six shillings and threepence, to a cabdriver to take us there, which he accepted. When we arrived we found that the hotel was not yet open for the season. Our driver frankly admitted that he was aware of this before we started from Clifton, but he thought "probably we knew better!" This not only aggravated the situation, but was a most unkind thrust, because we did not pretend to know anything about it—we only asked if he would drive us to the hotel for the figure above mentioned, and of course we took it for granted that it was open all the year round, as no intimation or hint had been previously given that the season only extended from June till September, and that they shut it up altogether during the rest of the year. There were one or two second-rate shoddy-looking lodging-houses near, but we never thought of going to them, as they did not appear tempting enough, so our cabman offered to drive us across the Suspension Bridge to the American side, a distance of less than half a mile, for another dollar, and we agreed. We found, however, we had to pay half a dollar more for toll dues for our carriage, but in the end we landed in an excellent hotel, "The Spencer House," Niagara City, where a capital dinner and a cigar helped to restore us to good humour.

In the cool of the evening we walked to the

Rapids above the Falls, and back to Prospect Point. It is simply impossible to describe one's feelings in witnessing this grand cataract for the first time. Even while sitting in the hotel, a quarter of a mile off, the roar of the water had a weird overpowering effect, and the whole town vibrated with the force of the torrent. The town of Niagara consists of large hotels, *bric-à-brac* and photograph stores, liquor saloons, and one or two grocery and drapers' stores.

The next morning by appointment, Mr. S——, a native of Niagara, whose acquaintance we made on the train between Kalamazoo and Detroit, called at our hotel to spend the day with us. He engaged a carriage-and-pair for us at four dollars for as long as we required it, very cheap for Niagara, so we started off in good style, Mr. S—— acting as "guide, philosopher, and friend."

First we drove across the bridge which spans the Rapids above the Falls, to Goat Island, which we drove round, stopping and getting out to look about us at various points of interest. For instance we descended the steps to the Cave o' the Winds, at the foot of the American Fall, and by-and-by crossed two or three little wooden bridges over small torrents which divide the Three Sister Islands, all of which we visited. Having returned from Goat Island to the mainland, we drew up at the incline railway at Prospect Point, and got into the little cable car, which descends by a very steep gradient, 170 feet, to the bed of the river. At the bottom we had a grand view of the American Fall, tumbling down with a continuous deafening thudding noise a few yards off from where we stood.

Our next move was across the Suspension Bridge to the Canadian side, where a mile upstream we alighted at the Horse-shoe Fall. This is by far the larger and prettier of the two cataracts. An attendant helped us to get into a suit of oilskins, for the hire of which we paid fifty cents each, and in this garb we descended again to the bed of the river in an elevator, and walked through the tunnel, which leads by a semicircle to an opening *right under* the Falls. Here we stood for some time fascinated, and with feelings quite indescribable, the curtain of water pouring down twelve or fifteen feet in front of us into the mass of foam and spray beneath. We felt on safer ground when we got back to the bank, but still would have been sorry to have missed such a strange experience.

A drive of two miles from the Horse-shoe Fall, the cantilever vehicular-and-railway-bridge combined is reached. Here we re-crossed to American territory, and two or three miles lower down the stream we arrived at the Whirlpool Rapids. Once more we made use of an elevator, and at the river side we had a splendid view of the Whirlpool with its boiling tumbling waters, rushing madly on through the narrow gorge, leaping into billows fifteen feet high, then falling and rising again, onward bounding in their majestic joyous struggle, as it were, for life and liberty. The Whirlpool is a grand spectacle, and in its own way is almost as fascinating as the Falls themselves. Verily there is only one Niagara in the world!

If I may be pardoned for offering advice to any who may visit Niagara, I would say, Don't attempt to see all that is worth seeing on foot. Hire a carriage, but make a firm bargain with the driver before starting, and don't pay until you are done with him; the fare ought not to exceed four dollars for the hire. You are sure to be pestered at the different places where you must leave the carriage to buy all sorts of curiosities that you do not want. *Don't buy anything.* Or mayhap you will be asked at every turn to have your photograph taken. *Don't!* You will be shown some beautiful photographs of the Falls mounted on cardboard, and an assurance given that your "counterfeit presentment" will be placed in the foreground of a similar one and sent to any address within a week. We were weak enough to allow ourselves to be taken (or should I say taken in?), for the pictures that were sent to us were miserable specimens of the photographic art. Besides, contrary to agreement, they were unmounted, and we only got possession of them the day before we sailed from New York homewards, I firmly believe, through the kind offices of our good friend Mr. S——.

These photographic swindlers get your money;

they never bargain for less than six photographs at a dollar each, and very frequently you hear no more about it. Do not, then, on any account encourage these 'cute Yankee rogues. I write this all the more confidently as the experiences of some of my friends have been exactly as stated above. I have no doubt we should have been pestered very much more than we were by *bric-à-brac* sellers if we had not been accompanied by our genial American friend, who was well known all over the neighbourhood, and to whom we were very much indebted for his kind courtesy.

CHAPTER XIII.

Departure from Niagara—Merritton Junction—Thorold—Electric Tramway—Hamilton—Arrival at Toronto—The University—Baseball—Toronto Island—Sunday in Toronto—Arrival at Ottawa.

OUR train left Niagara Falls Station at 7.20 a.m. *en route* for TORONTO. At the Suspension Bridge junction we had to change to the cars of the Grand Trunk Line in order to reach Port Dalhousie, on Lake Ontario, whence we intended getting the steamer across the lake to Toronto, a passage of three or four hours in ordinary favourable weather conditions.

On arriving at Merritton Junction we were told to change cars for Port Dalhousie, so we got out; this was about a quarter past eight in the morning. On making inquiry as to how long we would have to wait for our train we were told two hours and a half, and we also learned that the steamer leaves Port Dalhousie at eight o'clock every morning, which meant that we could not reach Toronto that day by this route. Nice muddle! but the railway officials at Niagara were entirely to blame for giving us wrong information.

There we were landed, or, I should say, stranded, at eight o'clock in the morning at a small wayside station, with not more than a score wooden houses and huts near; no hotel, only a dirty unpatronized-looking public-house, and the choice left us of either going on to Port Dalhousie at 10.45 a.m., and spending the day and night there, or waiting till 3 p.m., when we could reach Toronto direct the same day by train. We decided on the latter course, and in the meantime walked to a very busy manufacturing town called Thorold, four or five miles off. It was a steady pull uphill all the way, and the day being very sultry, and the road several inches deep with dust, we were glad when we reached the comfortable little hostelry at the top of the main street of the town. There we moistened our parched throats with a glass of cool and refreshing lager beer, which we enjoyed so much that M—— wished his neck were two feet long, so delicious was the sensation of getting his thirst satisfied at this particular time! an exclamation escaped from both of us simultaneously to the effect that it was "the finest beer in the world; yes, sir!" We had just got comfortably seated in the hotel parlour upstairs when the sky became overcast with one heavy black cloud. A very violent thunderstorm ensued, accompanied by a heavy downpour which lasted for three hours without a stop. Very welcome rain! for the country needed it badly.

The electric light is in use in Thorold, and tram-cars propelled by electricity run from there to

St. Catherine's, another thriving town seven miles off. As the route of the tramway lay viâ Merritton we took this conveyance back to the station.

The ship canal which connects Lakes Huron and Ontario passes through Thorold, and it was curious to see large three-masted ships gliding along on their passage from one lake to the other in what appeared at a distance to be only a field.

Our train was up to time, so at 3 p.m. we got "aboord." We stopped ten minutes at Hamilton, Ont., a large manufacturing city, which to all appearance was worthy of a visit, but our arrangements not permitting we hurried on, and Toronto was reached at half-past six o'clock. The Queen's Hotel, where we stayed, is a most comfortable one, and has the best situation of any in Toronto, as it overlooks Lake Ontario. The Royal Arms of Britain were emblazoned over the dining-room door, so in this and other ways we were not allowed to forget we were again on British soil.

Toronto is considered one of the handsomest cities on the American continent, and I am willing to concede it is at least one of the prettiest. Some streets are handsome, wide, and with splendid stone buildings on either side. Yonge Street and King Street are the chief business thoroughfares. Chemists and candy stores are plentiful; liquor saloons are few. These latter are compelled by law to close on Saturday at 7 p.m. till Monday morning. Hotel bars are shut at the same time, but guests can have what liquor they want by retiring to their room and having it sent there.

We had a number of calls to make, and, amongst others, we went to the address of Mr. C. J. M——, one of our fellow-voyagers in the *Anchoria*. Mr. M. had gone to Brockville, but his uncle, Mr. W. K——, one of Toronto's merchant princes, gave us an invitation to spend Sunday afternoon at his house, which we accepted. We then inspected the University[*] and museum, a handsome pile of buildings, the erection of which cost £300,000 not a great many years ago. An old classfellow of the writer's at the Royal High School of Edinburgh is Professor of Zoology here. Unfortunately he was at Ottawa, so we did not see him.

After lunch the day succeeding our arrival, we took a tramcar to the extreme outskirts of the city, as far as the recreation grounds, where we witnessed for the first time a great match at baseball played by two famous teams. A gentleman sitting next to us on the stand explained the various points of the game, and we were greatly interested in it. We never saw such splendid catching, fielding, or running at any cricket match—and we have seen many of the crack county teams in England en-

[*] Part of this magnificent building, with the museum and library, was burnt in February, 1890, damage to the extent of £100,000 being caused by the fire.

gaged in friendly rivalry with bat and ball—so we are not surprised that baseball has taken such a hold on Americans and Canadians. Played as it was on the occasion I refer to, it has all the elements of interest for an onlooker; but, like cricket, you require to know or get pointed out to you the fine bits of play in order to better enjoy watching the game. The only feature about baseball that I dislike is that *all* the players who take part in these public matches are professionals, who are paid very high salaries for their services. This fact to my mind takes away a good deal from the element of sport for sport's sake alone, which bulks so largely in the composition of the ordinary Britisher. In many cases these American and Canadian teams are got together by speculators for the sole purpose of making money, and some of the individual players earn as much as 1000 to 2500 dollars for a five months' engagement.

One lovely evening during our stay we hired a double pair-oared skiff, in which we paddled a couple of miles across the lake to Toronto Island, returning by moonlight. The whole scene was like fairyland; the water was smooth as a mirror, and a great number of small boats and yachts dotted its surface, whilst the electric light on the Island and in the town of Toronto, shining here and there amongst the trees, lent a charm to the scene which it will be difficult for us to forget.

On the Sunday, as arranged, we paid our visit to Mr. K——, who, with Mrs. K—— and family, received us most cordially, and entertained us with the kindest hospitality. They live in College Street, a beautiful avenue in the north-western suburbs of the city. Mr. K—— came from Scotland thirty-five years ago, and is now one of the wealthiest men in Toronto. We accompanied him and two of his daughters to the Presbyterian church which they attend, and heard a very strong defence of the Protestant as against the Roman Catholic religion. The sermon, we were told, had a special reference to a public question which was agitating the political world of Canada at the time.

Sunday in Toronto is kept in ultra-Scotch fashion. The public-houses are shut, as before mentioned, and the authorities are altogether behind the age in refusing to allow the Tramway Company to run a few cars on Sunday, for distances are much too great to permit of persons living in one part of the city to visit friends in another part, without great inconvenience. On this particular Sunday we would gladly have availed ourselves of the use of a car or a cab if it could have been got, but none were to be seen at the usual stances, the distance from our hotel being nearly three miles.

The lake navigation for passenger steamers was not yet opened for the season, so we missed what is always spoken of as a most delightful trip, a sail down the St. Lawrence, through the world-famed

Thousand Islands, and were obliged to go on to Ottawa by train. The weather had been magnificent, and there had hardly been any ice to speak of during winter, so we failed to see why summer arrangements should not have been begun earlier.; but that no doubt was just one of the many grumbles indulged in by the traveller when things go wrong somehow, or when he doesn't get his own way!

We left Toronto by Grand Trunk Railway at a quarter to nine in the morning, and arrived at OTTAWA at six o'clock evening. Ottawa is very romantically situated, being all ups and downs, like Edinburgh. The Government Offices and Houses of Parliament are a magnificent range of buildings, and are a credit to Canada and Great Britain. They are only distant a hundred yards from Russell House, the hotel we stayed at, and stand in the centre of beautiful grounds, bounded on one side by a cliff 200 feet high, overlooking the River Ottawa. The view to be got from various points along the top of the cliff is splendid. Woodlands, pasture lands, and distant mountains stretch out before you in magnificent panoramic form bounded by the far-off horizon. The lumber yards and sawmills in close proximity to the Chaudière Falls, add a sort of practical touch to the picture, although they detract considerably from its beauty as a landscape. The remainder of the evening of our one-day's visit to the capital of the Dominion of Canada we spent strolling round the suburbs amongst some charming villa residences and up and down pretty avenues. We also inspected the barracks, drill hall, and exercise ground of the militia before darkness compelled us to retrace our steps to the hotel.

CHAPTER XIV.

Departure from Ottawa—The River—Rideau Hall—Lumber Rafts—Montebello Château—Grenville—Carillon—First Railway in Canada—St. Ann's—Canadian Boat Song—Lachine Rapids—Montreal.

E left Ottawa by steamer at seven o'clock in the morning and arrived at Montreal at six o'clock at night. We found this a delightful trip, and a very agreeable change from the long journeys by train; although, taking it all over, the travelling from Chicago had been as comfortable as railway travelling could be. Soon after getting under weigh we glided past Rideau Hall, the residence of the Governor-General of Canada, and, close by, the château of Sir John Macdonald, Prime Minister of the Dominion. Both are beautifully situated high up on the right bank. The Ottawa is a very pretty stream, especially the first fifty miles we sailed down to a place called Grenville. The banks on both sides all along this part are thickly wooded, and many islands intercept the course of the river's flow. In summer these pretty shaded islets are thickly populated by parties of young fellows, who spend their holidays camping out, boating, and fishing. Between Ottawa and Montreal the river varies in

width from a quarter of a mile at Chaudière Falls, gradually widening until its waters mingle with the mighty St. Lawrence, a little above the Lachine Rapids, where it attains its greatest breadth, fifteen miles. The lumber trade is the chief industry of the whole district traversed by the river. We passed several large lumber establishments with sawmills, &c., where the trees are cut into logs and planks for shipment abroad. These logs are fastened together into immense rafts, some of which are a hundred yards square, and are towed down the river by small screw tug boats. When they reach the rapids below Grenville they are shot through in small portions, re-united lower down, and so on over the rapids at Lachine and on to Montreal, whence they are shipped to Europe, chiefly to Greenock and Liverpool.

We met a fine old gentleman on board the *Empress*, Mr. John Archibald Cameron, who is one of the big lumbermen of Ottawa. His grandfather was a Scotchman who fled to Canada from the United States when they threw off the British yoke. Mr. Cameron had never visited the land of his forefathers, but he evinced a great interest in the answers we supplied to the various queries he put with reference to Scotland. He had ample knowledge of her past history, and Scott and Burns were familiar friends; but his extraordinary anxiety to know what was going on at the present time, and his almost sentimental affection for a country he had never seen, but which he could not resist calling *home,* was very touching.

Montebello Château, the residence of Papineau, the chief of the French rebellion of 1837–38, was pointed out to us by the captain of our steamer, who was a very agreeable fellow, and showed us marked courtesy all through the trip. Papineau died some years ago, but his son now resides at the château in comparative retirement from public life.

At GRENVILLE we took train for Carillon, thirteen miles lower down the river. In the tourist season the steamers shoot the rapids between Grenville and Carillon, but it costs so much money in lock dues to work their way back that they only do it when there is sufficient traffic to make it pay. The little railway line between these two places was made in 1856, and is the first that was opened in this district of British North America. The very first railway made in Canada is that between St. John and La Prairie, thirty or forty miles south of Montreal, and was opened for traffic in 1840. The captain of the *Empress* is a son of the contractor who constructed it.

At CARILLON we got on board another steamer, the *Princess,* and from here the river widens considerably (the narrowest part being about three miles across) until it forms the junction with the St. Lawrence.

Some little time after leaving Carillon we

reached St. Ann's, where we were made fast to the pier for ten minutes, discharging goods and passengers. There is another rapid here, but we did not shoot it; our steamer took the smoother and safer passage through a splendid granite built lock, under a beautiful bridge, part of the Canadian Pacific line, which crosses the river at this point. This pretty village of St. Ann's is the place where Thomas Moore lived for some time; the house he stayed in was pointed out to us. It was here he composed the well-known Canadian boat song:—

"Row, brothers, row, the stream runs fast,
The rapids are near and the daylight's past."

It is a curious fact that the majority of the passengers, most of the crew of the steamer, and all the pier porters spoke nothing but French. Further down we passed some interesting villages inhabited almost exclusively by Red Indians, who earn a living by making La Crosse racquets.

The Rapids of Lachine were reached at 5.30 p.m., where we disembarked and took the train to Montreal, arriving shortly after 6 p.m. After dinner we walked down Ste Catherine Street for about two miles, and here again we observed that the French language predominated. The "Windsor," where we put up at, is one of the finest hotels on the American continent. The entrance hall appeared to us to be almost as large as the Royal Exchange, Glasgow. The "Palmer House" and

MONTREAL.

"Grand Pacific" in Chicago are the only two hotels that we saw during our travels that will compare with the Windsor for size and luxury. We had a letter of introduction to Mr. H——, who kindly devoted half a day to us, showing us the chief sights of the city. He told us we had walked right into the French quarter by going down Ste Catherine Street, which accounted for the amount of French conversation we had heard during our stroll the previous evening. Half of the population of Montreal are French, one-fifth Irish, and the remainder English, Scotch, and other nationalities. As to religion, two-thirds are Roman Catholics and one-third Protestant. There are a great many handsome buildings of grey marble or granite, in fact the entire city is built of one or the other. The Post Office and Notre Dame Cathedral are particularly noteworthy.

A day or two after our arrival we walked by a pretty path to the summit of the hill called Mount Royal Park, which stands 700 feet above the mean level of the city. It covers many hundred acres of ground, thickly wooded, the trees being of great variety and luxuriant growth. The summit is reached by several footpaths similar to the one we used, and there is also a well-made carriage drive, which winds round the hill to the top. On one side of the mountain a cable railway is in operation, the car running at regular intervals conveying passengers up and down at the moderate charge of five cents each. At the top there is erected a wooden observatory, access to which is got by ascending a series of flights of ladder stairs. From here we obtained a splendid view of Montreal and the River St. Lawrence, with the three-miles-long Victoria Tubular Bridge spanning it. This bridge was until recently the longest in the world, and was opened by the Prince of Wales on his first visit to Canada about twenty-five years ago. The city of Montreal stands on an island, seventeen miles long, formed by the St. Lawrence dividing into two streams a little above Lachine, and reuniting into one grand river lower down. From our exalted position we could see the water-line all round.

After walking through the English cemetery—there is also a French cemetery in the park, but we had not time to visit it—on our way back to town we stumbled across the golf links. We followed two players, who were average specimens of the novice at this grand game. Their enthusiasm, however, made up for the want of skill. After a casual remark addressed to M—— by one of the players, we got on quite friendly terms when they learned that we too were devotees of the royal and ancient game. At the conclusion of the "round" we were invited into the clubhouse, which is a comfortable pavilion, and we pledged each other in a "drop o' Scotch." We were then invited to make up a "foursome." My friend M—— declined, modestly protesting that he made a better spectator of, than an active participator in, the game; but I, not unwillingly, availed myself of the pleasure of playing two rounds, or eighteen holes, partnered with the Rev. J. B—— against Dr. S——- and the club professional. The course is only a second rate one, owing to the nature of the turf, and the fact that there is a good deal of stony ground to be met with. The putting greens also might be better; still, considering all the disadvantages our brother golfers in Montreal labour under, from the limited number they can draw from to get players, and the difficulty they must have in keeping the club in a prosperous condition in a country where golf is almost unknown, they are to be congratulated on having a course at all. Many sons of Britain are thus thrown together who might otherwise never have become acquainted in the land of their adoption, and memories of home are kept alive and friendships formed, and at the same time healthful exercise got, which, but for the golf links, would have been impossible of attainment.

After the game we returned to the club-house, and here we noticed a face we felt certain we had seen before, but where we had not the remotest idea. Whenever the gentleman I refer to spoke, we recognized the east of Scotland accent. He was Mr. F. B——, who at one time had a private school in the Grange Road, Edinburgh, but went to Canada with Mr. J. L. J—— (now the manager of a large meat extract company whose headquarters are in London) when the Canadian Meat Company was started, lost all his money in the concern, which burst up in a few years, and he is now an exporter of produce. He called at the Windsor at night, and we spent a very pleasant evening together. He had ever so many questions to ask about old friends and everything political and social connected with " dear old Scotland."

CHAPTER XV.

Departure from Montreal—Arrival at Plattsburg—Lake Champlain—Saratoga—Boston.

WE learned that the steamers on Lakes Champlain and St. George were not running yet for the season, so were obliged to travel to Saratoga all the way by rail instead of, as we intended, having a pleasant variety in the shape of a sail down these famous lakes.

This being the third disappointment of a similar nature we had experienced, compels me to advise the intending tourist to visit the States and Canada at a somewhat later period of the year than we did. The best time to start from this side is about the beginning or middle of August. The heat in July and early August is very severe, but generally splendid weather follows for a couple of months, as the Fall, or Indian Summer, lasts till the end of October.

Before leaving Montreal we called on Professor J. C. M.——, D.D., a native of Paisley, to whom we had a letter of introduction, and spent a very agreeable hour with him. He has been resident a number of years in Montreal, and is a professor in M'Gill College there. We also inspected St.

Peter's Cathedral, a massive Roman Catholic church, built after the model of St. Peter's, Rome, but on a smaller scale. It will be another year at least before it is entirely finished, but worship is now regularly held in a part of the interior. Montreal strikes a stranger as being famous for three things—the number of priests and French people one meets, and the great number of handsome churches of all denominations.

The hotel porter got our baggage passed through the Customs before starting on our journey southwards, so we were saved any unnecessary bother on that score. It is very troublesome to travellers to be obliged to open up their trunks and have them inspected every time the frontier is passed into the States or *vice versâ*. At a place like Niagara or Detroit, which are on the borders, so to speak, of Canada, it is a double grievance.

In a three and a half hours' journey from Montreal our train reached PLATTSBURG. This pretty little town lies on the shore of Lake Champlain, and the hotel we stopped at, the "Fouquet House," faces the lake. The population is 10,000, and the chief industry is tinplating. A pleasant stroll in the evening revealed to us the usual pretty avenues we have met with everywhere, the trees forming a shelter alike from winter storms and summer sun. On the way here the general aspect of the country is very significant. In Canada the farms are small, and the land is not nearly so well cultivated, at least it has a more unkempt look until you pass the frontier line at Rouse's Point, where a marked change is noticeable. In this respect, as in every other of a business kind, the American appears to be ahead of the Canadian, although I should say the latter enjoys life much better with his shorter working hours, his Saturday half-holiday, and his Sunday rest.

Next day before leaving for Saratoga, we wandered along the shore of the lake, the appearance of which at Plattsburg bears a striking resemblance to the Firth of Clyde as seen from the West Bay, Dunoon. It is five miles across here, but the width varies from twelve miles, at its broadest part, to a hundred yards, at the upper and lower ends. Its extreme length is 115 miles, so although it is reckoned a very small sheet of water in America, it would be considered a very extensive one in this country. Lake St. George is, I imagine, about half the size of Lake Champlain. The railroad to Saratoga runs through a well-cultivated rich bit of country, skirting these lakes a considerable part of the way. A hilly district, in which a good deal of iron ore and marble is found, is also traversed *en route*. The journey, which occupied five hours altogether, was a very pleasant one, but gradually we seemed to be nearing warmer latitudes, and when we landed in SARATOGA we had the curiosity to examine a thermometer, and were not surprised to find that it indicated 88° in the shade. Whew!

after the cool weather in Montreal we took badly with this sort of temperature, although thankful enough it was no worse, as it frequently rises to 95°, and even higher, in midsummer.

Saratoga, the gay Indian summer or "Fall" resort of wealthy Americans, is just a city of hotels, a series of lofty wooden buildings with verandahs canopied in some instances at the third storey, stretching along one after the other down the main thoroughfare. Some of them can accommodate 1000 guests comfortably, but many were not yet opened for the season, which extends from June till September. If one of these hotels took fire, the whole town would be laid in ashes, at least that thought occurred to M—— and myself more than once during our stay.

There are more than thirty mineral springs in various parts of the town, all under cover and let to tenants, or perhaps in some cases the proprietor takes charge himself. You go into a shop which looks like a British Workman's Refreshment Room, and there you see the water bubbling up into a marble font. The usual charge for a tumblerful is one cent. There is also a spring in the Congress Park, at which you may drink *gratis*. This park, with its lakes and shady walks, and bandstand and recreation hall, must be a gay scene when fully patronized during the season.

One evening we went to the theatre, where a third-rate performance of "Leah" was going on,

but we did not sit it out. Placards were hung up
in different parts of the interior with the bare but
suggestive announcement, "Gentlemen will not
spit on the floor." And yet I regret to say that I
cannot truthfully record the fact that the spittoons,
which were plentifully scattered about, received
any better patronage than usual. Between each
act a bill was suspended in front of the curtain
advertising the merits of the "Royal Mineral
Spring Water," samples of which in tumblers
were handed round the audience, for which no
charge was made.

We left Saratoga at 7.25 a.m. and arrived at
Boston at 3.30 p.m., as dusty as millers and as
"hot as rolls and gravy." The thermometer
registered 87° in the shade, and it must have
been ten degrees warmer inside the sunbaked cars.
Fortunately the route lay in the midst of beautiful
scenery nearly all the way, by mountain, forest,
lake, and river. On emerging from the Hoosac
Tunnel, five miles long, cut right through the
Hoosac Mountains, we struck the river Deerfield,
whose course we followed for forty or fifty miles.
The train then entered a fertile valley, through
which the river Connecticut flows, and followed
its windings for many miles more. The Pass of
Killiecrankie is the only bit of scenery I know of
that will compare with this part of our journey—
the little towns of Charlemont, Shelbourne Falls,
and Athol are lovely spots that will linger long

in the memory of any who has seen them. If
the mountains were higher the comparison with
the Highland Railway of Scotland would be
unique—but in all other respects the similarity is
striking.

The home of *literati*, the "Hub" or centre of
civilization, as it is sometimes called—BOSTON—
every one knows to be one of the oldest cities in
America. The streets are built in all directions,
having seemingly been curved and crescented as
passing whim dictated. It is interesting in a
strange town to walk about noting the different
types of men and women you meet, for the inhabitants of every separate city are stamped with some
particular characteristic which distinguishes them,
in however slight a degree, from their fellows.
Here we appeared to be transported from America
to, say, Liverpool; everything—the streets, houses,
buildings—and everybody looked more English
like than in any of the other towns we had visited
during our tour. The Irish are a strong body
here, and control the government of the city in
matters municipal. There is also a considerable
Chinese population, who have a monopoly, as
usual, of the laundry business. By accident we
stumbled into the Chinese quarter amongst a crowd
of several hundreds of these innocent-looking,
blandly-smiling Celestials, who were lounging
around their doorsteps smoking cigarettes and
talking in their peculiar "click-ya" native tongue.

They were all clean and respectably dressed in native costume. They speak so quietly, and move about so softly, and evidently behave themselves as good citizens ought, that I rather admire John Chinaman, and sympathize a good deal with him when I find him trying to push his fortune in a foreign land. There appears to me to be some of the enterprise of a Scotsman in his composition, and on that ground alone, if on no other, he deserves our sympathy.

The Sunday during our sojourn in Boston was a terrible day of desecration. In the morning we went by tramcar to City Point, three miles distant from our hotel—the " United States "—where we had an opportunity of seeing the Brighton of Boston, with its fine pier and restaurants, all of which are conducted on temperance principles. Hundreds of pleasure-seekers were crowded on the beach, promenading the pier and rowing and sailing in all sorts and sizes of small boats and yachts, and they seemed to be getting possibly as much good in this way as probably sleeping in church on such a warm Sunday. In the afternoon we returned to the city and got on board the three-decked river steamer *General Lincoln*, and enjoyed a sail of twenty miles down the bay, which is dotted all over with pretty islands, to Nantasket Beach. There must have been from 1500 to 2000 people on board, a most respectable orderly crowd, of which perhaps two-thirds were men. Many of the passengers went ashore at Nantasket to return to Boston later, but some came back, as we did, in the same steamer, our trip occupying rather more than four hours, so we arrived at our hotel in good time for supper at 6 p.m. In the evening we went to the Boston Theatre in Washington Street, which was well filled with a class of people similar to those we met on the steamer, except that the gentle sex predominated this time. The performance was of the miscellaneous concert kind, commencing with an overture by a good orchestra, followed by solos and duets from operas, &c. In the second part a chorus of 200 voices, with the orchestra and a quartette of soloists, gave a fine rendering of Rossini's "Stabat Mater," which concluded the entertainment; and so ended an eventful Sunday.

Our experience as related above is the usual Sabbath observance by a large class of Bostonians, and it is not my province to attempt to argue the question of whether it is right or wrong. We in Scotland certainly hold very different ideas of how Sunday should be spent, but it is idle to ignore the fact that our country is a very small speck in the vast universe, and therefore it is unlikely that we have been endowed with all the wisdom necessary to draw a hard and fast line between right and wrong in the conduct of individuals and communities on the Day of Rest. To look at it from a utilitarian point of view, I am inclined to ask, and with this query I dismiss the subject, if it is not just possible that we have allowed tradition and custom to chain us too long to methods which, however excellent in themselves, often prove highly inconvenient?

CHAPTER XVI.

Boston—Baseball—Fall River—The Steamer *Providence*—Long Island Sound—Arrival at New York.

WE were fortunate enough to be in Boston when a baseball match took place between two of the eight champion teams of America, the "Boston" and the "Cleveland." A great crowd assembled, the grand stands being packed, and some splendid play was shown. Unluckily the game had to be abandoned when only half finished owing to a sudden heavy downpour of rain, which soaked the ground so thoroughly that further play was impossible. In the evening of the same day we left Boston at six o'clock by train for FALL RIVER, where we arrived in a little less than an hour, and got on board the *Providence*, one of the magnificent American river steamers which one sometimes hears about, but must be seen to be appreciated.

If two *Ionas* or *Columbas*, so familiar to tourists and pleasure-seekers in the West of Scotland, were joined together alongside, and other two placed on the top of them, the interior of the whole opened up from the main deck to the skylights, with galleries running round inside and out from stem to stern, some idea of the size of these magnificent floating palaces might be got. The *Providence* is 87 feet broad, and about 350 feet long. The *Pilgrim* is the same, whilst the *Puritan* is still larger, measuring 95 feet broad and long in proportion. All three belong to the Fall River Line.

Until we got inside Long Island Sound the sea was rough and the motion uncomfortable, these huge light-draught pleasure boats not being intended for dirty weather; but the latter part of the passage was smooth and enjoyable enough, so far as the motion of the vessel was concerned, only unfortunately it was wet overhead, and so foggy that we missed a good deal of the view. On a bright moonlight night these trips must be most entrancing, as the scenery is said to be very fine. We had 1000 passengers on board, and berths were provided for each. By paying one dollar extra we got a state-room, owing to some one not turning up. I ought to have said the steamers on this route only sail during the night—there is no daylight service. There are 400 state-rooms in each vessel, and those who "know the ropes" secure one by paying a dollar, over and above the regular first-class fare, at the depôt at Boston or at the wharf at New York early in the morning of the day the steamer sails. They are always over-applied for, so it was the merest accident that gave us this luxury. A fine string orchestra accompanies each steamer, and plays a selection of music in the saloon from 7.30 till 10.30 every evening.

We arrived at the wharf at New York at nine o'clock next morning, and profiting by our previous experience of New York cabbies, took the Elevated to Forty-second Street, and then got a tramcar to the Grand Union Hotel, which now appeared quite a familiar quarter. We had travelled by rail over 3000 miles, and our two steamer trips on the river Ottawa and from Fall River to New York, added 300 miles more. Most of our journeys having been taken by day we saw a great deal of the country besides the places we actually stopped at. During the week we spent in New York before embarking for home we had ample opportunity to inspect what we had not time to overtake during the first few days after our arrival. The Stock Exchange and other places of interest down town; the Central Park, to which we devoted an entire day, and it was well worth it; Brooklyn, with its many fine churches and its picturesque park, were each visited, and we also spent a day at Gravesend, Long Island. Besides, we also found time to gather up the impressions we had formed during our scamper, and the information we had gleaned of American institutions, habits, and customs, and these are reserved for the next chapter.

CHAPTER XVII.

Impressions of America—Methods of Government—Bribery—Politics—Administration of Justice—Jury-packing—Habits and Customs—Express Companies—Railway "Check" System—Systems of Heating—Management of Crowds—Investments in Land—Homeward Bound.

IN many things we have much to learn from our American cousins, in some they might learn a great deal from us. Their political ways and methods of municipal government are unsatisfactory. There are too many men amongst them who are greedy for office, and are not particular in the means they use to obtain preferment; and it is almost unnecessary to add, such men are scandalously unscrupulous when they get into power. It was admitted by every American we met that there is an amount of bribery and corruption in every department of the Government and administration of the country that is appalling to a Britisher. For instance, when a municipality has a contract for paving or some kindred job to give out, the man who can bribe the patrons heaviest has the best chance of securing the work; and the long-suffering American citizen, who, as a rule, is too anxiously coining dollars at his business to give much attention to other matters, has to pay more money in taxation than he ought to, and the work is scamped or indifferently done, to enable the contractors to earn a profit at all. This was one of the explanations given to us to account for the disgraceful state of the streets in many of the cities we visited. One well-known glaring monument of jobbery and robbery is the white marble Court House of New York, which, I believe, cost £6,000,000 sterling, two-thirds of which amount disappeared mysteriously into the pockets of contractors and others.

With regard to the two great political parties of America, I cannot say that I grasped the full significance of the difference between Democrats and Republicans. One thing, however, is certain, that the former wish to reform the tariff in the direction of Free Trade, whilst the latter believe in Protection. It goes without saying that the great majority of the manufacturers, who alone have anything to gain by opposing the free and unfettered importation of the manufactured goods of other nations, are Republicans; but Free Trade principles are slowly but surely finding favour amongst the toiling millions. A country that has already adopted a system of manhood suffrage and free education will, I feel assured, not be very long in throwing off the Protection nightmare, and wake up to see the enormous benefit a policy of Free Trade would confer on the great masses of her citizens.

Politics is a distinct profession, and has its devotees just as much as medicine and law, and for this reason the members of legislature all receive salaries. When a change takes place in the presidency every official in Government service, from members of the cabinet down to petty judges, post-office clerks, customs' officers, and even policemen, get their *congé* to make way for men who belong to the political party which is in power for the time being. This system works very badly, I think, in the foreign and diplomatic service, where ambassadors and consuls, instead of being, as they ought to be, the representatives of the whole nation, sink into the position of being merely the nominees of a political party. However eminent they may be, and no matter how well fitted in every respect for the posts they occupy, they are invariably recalled at a change of administration, and their places filled by men who, according to our idea, are just beginning to learn their ambassadorial duties when they too, in the course of political events, have to give place to other new and untried successors. The entire system of changing Government officials in such a drastic manner is wrong, and cannot work either economically or advantageously for the nation which adopts it.

Much might be said, too, against the administration of justice. Many of the petty judges, as I have said, are removable at a change of administration, and we heard several Americans say that every judge has his price, excepting perhaps those in the higher courts of the country. We were even told that in some States, particularly in the West, if a man were arrested on a charge of murder he would certainly get off if his purse was long enough! In several States it is the easiest thing possible to pack a jury, there being plenty of loafers who earn their living by acting as jurymen. All that is required is to arrange with the sergeant in charge of the Court House to bring in a dozen men you have collected outside, and who, for a consideration, will return a verdict whichever way you want! A case in point happened in Kalamazoo a little while before we arrived, where the foreman in a factory was locked up for assault. Had he been found guilty, as he ought to have been, for the assault was clearly proved, he might have been sentenced to two years' imprisonment; but, being a valuable workman, the business of the firm which employed him would have seriously suffered had such a catastrophe occurred, so his master packed the jury in the manner described above, a verdict of not guilty was returned in the teeth of the clearest evidence, and the foreman was forthwith restored to liberty and usefulness.

I have already alluded to the habit of smoking and chewing indulged in by the majority of Americans, and I shall now add a few words with reference to their eating and drinking. Brother Jonathan seems to prefer to have his dinner cold, for he orders it all at once, and soup, fish, *entrées*, vegetables, joints, and sweets, are brought in all together, and spread out in small dishes in front of him. As a rule he has a good appetite, and eats fast. He dips into all his dishes in the most promiscuous way, and only one plate is provided until the sweets are attacked, when another is forthcoming. This plan certainly saves the time of the waiter, but any casual observer cannot help seeing that a great amount of waste is the result, because in hotels conducted on the American plan you can order every dish on the *menu*, if so inclined, and generally far more is ordered than partaken of. On the other hand, Americans are very temperate so far as taking alcoholic drink is concerned. It was quite a rare thing to see any wine or beer at *table d'hôte*. If any stimulant be taken it is generally in the form of a " cocktail " or " appetiser," which they drink at the bar before proceeding to the dining-room. The great majority, however, drink nothing but water, and that they must have at every meal—breakfast, dinner, and supper, in a large tumbler containing one or more lumps of ice. At breakfast fruit is eaten the first thing, and as a rule it enters more largely into the diet of our cousins across the Atlantic than with us.

Americans are of such go-ahead nature that they adopt a new invention and give it a trial almost as soon as discovered. They never care what the cost will be, if they think it a good thing. I have made mention of quite small towns where electric tramways are running, and where the electric light is in full use, a proof of enterprise which is developed to a much larger extent in all directions in big cities. We noticed an ingenious contrivance in New York which escaped our observation, if it be in use, elsewhere. I refer to the Switching Tramway rail. At a junction a small iron plate is fixed in the ground somewhat on the same principle as those in use in front of weighing houses. When a car is required to go on to another line of rails, the driver does not stop and get off and shift the points as they do here; he merely pulls his horses slightly to one side, so that one of them treads on the plate, and the car switches on to the branch line itself. It is a clever invention, and works with absolute certainty.

The Express system is a great institution in America, and is largely taken advantage of by every one. A great number of companies similar to our Globe Parcel Express carry on an extensive business in receiving, despatching, and delivering parcels or boxes to all parts of a city, or to any part of the country. Express men meet the arrival of steamers and trains, "touting" for business, and generally it is very convenient to hand over your luggage to a servant of one of these companies to be forwarded to your hotel or home. You pay a small sum, for which a receipt is given, and if the package does not arrive all right (but it seldom miscarries) the company whose receipt you hold is responsible for the loss. In New York you can "express" to any part of the city a parcel as big as you like, from a handbag to a Saratoga trunk, for the uniform charge of fifty cents.

Another great convenience to the traveller in America is the luggage "check" system, which all the railroad companies have adopted. No trouble is experienced in being obliged to look after your traps as with us here. By leaving orders with the clerk at the hotel to get certain packages "checked" through to the town you are going to, and by having your railway ticket exhibited along with them, you are saved all further anxiety on their account, and have nothing to pay in excess of the ordinary fare for your journey. The official in charge at the Baggage Department at the Railroad Depôt gives you a brass tablet or "check" with a number on it, and fixes with a strap on to your box a duplicate of the brass tablet he has given you. When you arrive at your destination you hand your check to the Express man, or else you may give it to the clerk at your hotel, who will despatch a porter for your luggage. Sometimes a trifling charge is made at the hotel for sending for it if the depôt is any distance away, but, as a rule, a small "tip" to the porter is all that is required.

To travel in America with comfort it is important to have as few packages as possible; rather have one large trunk than two small ones, because, as a rule, at railway stations you have to be your own porter. These useful officials consider themselves quite as good as you—and why not? so they are generally above earning an honest sixpence by carrying your portmanteau along the platform. You can get your things washed and dressed in hotels at a few hours notice, so you do not require to burden yourself with too much underclothing. Hat-boxes are unnecessary, as plenty of racks are fitted up in the cars where you can place your satin hat whilst wearing your travelling one. A small handbag, which you can conveniently carry, is to be recommended in addition to your portmanteau. In summer time travelling is such dusty work that a linen dust coat is absolutely necessary if you do not wish your clothes to be completely spoiled; and, if the weather be warm, a celluloid collar, and cuffs of the same material, will be found both cool and comfortable to wear.

A great number of private houses are heated by hot-air or steam pipes in place of stoves, thus saving labour, and at the same time having the advantage of cleanliness. All the hotels we were in were heated in one or other of these ways. I am old-fashioned enough, however, to prefer the cheery fireplace with its glowing embers; but doubtless the severity of the American winter renders a more all-round method of distributing warmth necessary.

On their manner of managing crowds who, say, are entering a theatre or booking their seats for a train at a railway station, one can have nothing but praise to bestow. A *queue* is formed by a policeman or official in attendance, and each one as he or she arrives has to take his place in the rear, and thus all are served in their proper order. There is no unseemly jostling or crushing, each one waits his turn patiently, and in the long run considerable time is saved and no discomfort felt by any.

Much money has already been made in America by judicious investments in land, and much more will be made in the future in the same way. It is easy to get $7\frac{1}{2}$ to 10 per cent. interest for loans with the best security. Cities spring up so quickly that one might, by a little foresight in securing "lots" in a district that is likely to develop, net a handsome return in a very few years.

There is no country in the world that has such immense possibilities before it, and peopled as it is by such an energetic race, and favoured by nature with so great a variety of climate, I see no reason why America should not, during the next twenty or thirty years, be not only "the biggest" but "the richest and best nation in the world; yes, sir!"

Embarking on the City of Rome, that most comfortable and commodious of Atlantic steamers,

Liverpool was reached after a smooth passage (with the exception of one day when, och! we had a storm) in a little more than a week from port to port. The saloon of this great steamer for two or three days after our departure was a mass of bloom, the tables being covered with baskets and bouquets of choicest flowers brought by loving hands of friends of passengers who had come to the wharf at New York to say " good bye." On the voyage we passed a derelict with not a sign of life on board, and a few days later we sailed within two miles of one of these beautiful monsters of the Atlantic, the greatest danger and terror to the intrepid mariner —a huge iceberg. We had also twenty-four hours of the inevitable fog, but during the remainder of the voyage fine weather prevailed. And so ended a most delightful scamper through some of the cities of America.

THE END.

PRINTED BY WILLIAM MACKENZIE, HOWARD STREET, GLASGOW

www.ingramcontent.com/pod-product-compliance
Lightning Source LLC
Chambersburg PA
CBHW020114170426
43199CB00009B/531